PERT MATH TEST SUCCESS

PERT Math Study Guide and Practice Tests

© COPYRIGHT 2008-2014. Academic Success Media DBA www.college-placement-test.com
All rights reserved. No part of this publication may be reproduced, stored in a retrieval system, or transmitted, in any form or by any means, electronic, mechanical, photocopying, recording, or otherwise.

COPYRIGHT NOTICE TO EDUCATORS: Please respect copyright law. Under no circumstances may you make copies of these materials for distribution to students. Should you wish to use the materials in a classroom, you are legally required to purchase a copy for each of your students.

Note: PERT and the Postsecondary Educational Readiness Test are trademarks of McCann Testing. Neither McCann Testing nor the Florida Department of Education are affiliated with or endorse this publication.

PERT Test Information

The Florida PERT (Postsecondary Educational Readiness Test) is a placement test that your college will administer in order to assess your mathematical, reading, and writing skills. The PERT is an untimed computer-adaptive test. This means that you will take the test on a computer and that your response to previous questions will determine the difficulty level of subsequent questions. In other words, if you are answering the questions correctly, the problems should become more difficult as the test progresses.

Test questions on the PERT are multiple-choice. Since the PERT is a secure test, the items in this book are not actual test questions. However, this practice material is designed to review the necessary mathematical skills covered on the PERT Exam by simulating the difficulty level and format of questions you may face on the actual test.

While you cannot pass or fail the PERT, your results from the exam will be used to place you into classes during your freshman year. If you perform poorly on the exam, you may need to take non-credit developmental classes that will cost you both time and money. It is therefore worthwhile to be well prepared for the examination.

How to Use this Publication

You should study the tips and example problems in the math concept and formula review in Part 1 of the book first.

While going through the study guide in Part 1, you should pay special attention to the exam tips, which are highlighted in the "A+" boxes.

When you have studied the tips and sample problems, you should then proceed to the practice tests in Part 2 of the book.

Please be sure to complete all three of the PERT math practice tests in this publication as each practice test increases in level of difficulty.

TABLE OF CONTENTS

Part 1 – Study Guide with Math Concept and Formula Review

Applying standard concepts: 1

Computations with Integers   2

Fractions: Multiplying Fractions   3

    Dividing Fractions   4

    Finding the Lowest Common Denominator (LCD)   5

    Simplifying Fractions   8

Mixed Numbers   9

PEMDAS – Order of Operations   11

Percentages and Decimals   14

Proportions   16

Ratios   17

Setting Up Basic Equations   18

Working with Averages   20

Algebra concepts and formulas:

The FOIL Method and Working with Polynomials   23

    Multiplying Polynomials Using the FOIL Method   23

    Dividing Polynomials Using Long Division   24

    Substituting Values in Polynomial Expressions   25

    Operations on Polynomials Containing Three Terms   25

Factoring Polynomials   26

    Basic Factoring   27

    Factoring – Advanced Problems   28

    Factoring to Find Possible Values of a Variable   32

Fractions Containing Fractions   33

Fractions Containing Radicals   34

Fractions Containing Rational Expressions   36

    Adding and Subtracting Fractions Containing Rational Expressions   36

Multiplying Fractions Containing Rational Expressions	37
Dividing Fractions Containing Rational Expressions	38
Inequalities	40
Laws of Exponents	42
Adding Exponents	43
Subtracting Exponents	44
Multiple Solutions	44
Practical Problems	46
Solving by Elimination	48
Solving for an Unknown Variable	49
Square Roots, Cube Roots, and Other Radicals	50
Factoring Radicals	50
Multiplication of Radicals	52
Rationalizing Radicals	53
Systems of Equations	54

Coordinate geometry concepts and formulas:

Distance Formula	57
Midpoints	58
Slope and Slope-Intercept	59
x and y intercepts	61

Part 2 – PERT Math Practice Tests

PERT Math Practice Test 1	63
PERT Math Practice Test 2	71
PERT Math Practice Test 3	78

Answers and Solutions to the PERT Math Practice Tests

PERT Math Practice Test 1 – Answers and Solutions	86
PERT Math Practice Test 2 – Answers and Solutions	104
PERT Math Practice Test 3 – Answers and Solutions	126

PART 1 – STUDY GUIDE WITH MATH CONCEPT AND FORMULA REVIEW

Applying Standard Concepts:

Although the PERT test will usually will not have questions covering standard concepts, students will be required to understand standard concepts in order to solve more complex problems on the exam. Students should therefore have a good understanding of the following basic mathematical skills:

- Computations with Integers
- Basic Operations with Fractions
- Basic Operations with Mixed Numbers
- Order of Operations
- Percentages and Decimals
- Proportions
- Ratios
- Setting Up Basic Equations
- Working with Averages

Please study the sample problems in this section if you need to refresh your skills in any of the above areas.

Computations with Integers

Computations with integers are assessed on the PERT examination.

Integers are positive and negative whole numbers. Integers cannot have decimals, nor can they be mixed numbers. In other words, they can't contain fractions.

One of the most important concepts to remember about integers is that two negative signs together make a positive number.

Why do two negatives make a positive? In plain English, you can think of it like using "not" two times in one sentence.

For example, you tell your friend: "I do not want you to not go to the party."

In the sentence above, you are really telling your friend that you want him or her to attend the party.

In other words, the "two negatives" concept in math is similar to the "two negatives" concept in the English language.

So, when you see a number like − (−2) you have to use 2 in your calculation.

Look at the example problem that follows.

Problem 1:

− (−5) + 3 = ?

A. −8

B. −2

C. 2

D. 8

The correct answer is D.

According to the concepts stated above, we know that − (−5) = 5

So, we can substitute this into the equation in order to solve it.

− (−5) + 3 = ?

5 + 3 = 8

A+ | Remember that when you see two negatives signs together, you need to make a positive number.

You will also see problems that ask you to perform multiplication or division on integers.

Some of these problems may ask you to find an integer that meets certain mathematical requirements, like in problem 2 below.

Problem 2:

What is the largest possible product of two even integers whose sum is 22?

A. 11

B. 44

C. 100

D. 120

The correct answer is D.

For problems that ask you to find the largest possible product of two even integers, first you need to divide the sum by 2.

The sum in this problem is 22, so we need to divide this by 2.

22 ÷ 2 = 11

Now take the result from this division and find the 2 nearest even integers that are 1 number higher and lower.

11 + 1 = 12

11 − 1 = 10

Then multiply these two numbers together in order to get the product.

12 × 10 = 120

Fractions – Multiplying

You will see problems on the exam that ask you to multiply fractions.

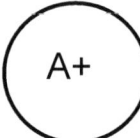 When multiplying fractions, multiply the numerators from each fraction. Then multiply the denominators.

The numerator is the number on the top of each fraction.

The denominator is the number on the bottom of the fraction.

Problem:

What is $\frac{1}{3} \times \frac{2}{3}$?

A. $\frac{2}{3}$

B. $\frac{2}{6}$

C. $\frac{2}{9}$

D. $\frac{1}{3}$

The correct answer is C.

Multiply the numerators.

1 × 2 = 2

Then multiply the denominators.

3 × 3 = 9

These numbers form the new fraction.

$\frac{2}{9}$

Fractions – Dividing

You will also need to know how to divide fractions for the exam.

 To divide fractions, invert the second fraction by putting the denominator on the top and numerator on the bottom. Then multiply.

Problem:

$$\frac{1}{5} \div \frac{4}{7} = ?$$

A. $\frac{4}{20}$

B. $\frac{7}{20}$

C. $\frac{4}{35}$

D. $\frac{5}{35}$

The correct answer is B.

Remember to invert the second fraction by putting the denominator on the top and the numerator on the bottom.

Our problem was: $\frac{1}{5} \div \frac{4}{7} = ?$

So the second fraction $\frac{4}{7}$ becomes $\frac{7}{4}$ when inverted.

Now use the inverted fraction to solve the problem.

$$\frac{1}{5} \div \frac{4}{7} =$$

$$\frac{1}{5} \times \frac{7}{4} = \frac{7}{20}$$

Fractions – Finding the Lowest Common Denominator (LCD)

In some fraction problems, you will have to find the lowest common denominator.

In other words, before you add or subtract fractions, you have to change them so that the bottom numbers in each fraction are the same.

You do this by multiplying the numerator [top number] by the same number you use on the denominator for each fraction.

 Remember to multiply the numerator and denominator by the same number when you are converting to the LCD.

Problem:

What is $\dfrac{1}{9} + \dfrac{9}{27}$?

A. $\dfrac{12}{27}$

B. $\dfrac{9}{27}$

C. $\dfrac{3}{27}$

D. $\dfrac{10}{36}$

The correct answer is A.

STEP 1: To find the LCD, you have to look at the factors for each denominator.

Factors are the numbers that equal a product when they are multiplied by each other.

So, the factors of 9 are:

1 × 9 = 9

3 × 3 = 9

The factors of 27 are:

1 × 27 = 27

3 × 9 = 27

STEP 2: Determine which factors are common to both denominators by comparing the lists of factors.

In this problem, the factors of 3 and 9 are common to the denominators of both fractions.

We can illustrate the common factors as shown.

We saw that the factors of 9 were:

1 × **9** = 9

3 × 3 = 9

The factors of 27 were:

1 × 27 = 27

3 × **9** = 27

So, the numbers in bold above are the common factors.

STEP 3: Multiply the common factors to get the lowest common denominator.

The numbers that are in bold above are then used to calculate the lowest common denominator.

3 × 9 = 27

So, the lowest common denominator (LCD) for each fraction above is 27.

STEP 4: Convert the denominator of each fraction to the LCD.

You convert the fraction by referring to the factors from step 3.

Multiply the numerator and the denominator by the same factor.

Our problem was $\dfrac{1}{9} + \dfrac{9}{27} = ?$

So, we convert the first fraction as follows:

$\dfrac{1}{9} \times \dfrac{3}{3} = \dfrac{3}{27}$

We do not need to convert the second fraction of $\dfrac{9}{27}$ because it already has the LCD.

STEP 5: When both fractions have the same denominator, you can perform the operation to solve the problem.

$$\frac{1}{9} + \frac{9}{27} =$$

$$\frac{3}{27} + \frac{9}{27} = \frac{12}{27}$$

Fractions – Simplifying

You will also need to know how to simplify fractions.

 To simplify fractions, look to see what factors are common to both the numerator and denominator.

In the example problem above, our result was $\frac{12}{27}$.

Problem:

Simplify: $\frac{12}{27}$

A. $\frac{1}{3}$

B. $\frac{3}{4}$

C. $\frac{3}{9}$

D. $\frac{4}{9}$

The correct answer is D.

STEP 1: Look at the factors of the numerator and denominator.

The factors of 12 are:

1 × 12 = 12

2 × 6 = 12

3 × 4 = 12

You will remember that the factors of 27 are:

1 × 27 = 27

3 × 9 = 27

So, we can see that the numerator and denominator have the common factor of 3.

STEP 2: Simplify the fraction by dividing the numerator and denominator by the common factor.

Our fraction in this problem is $\frac{12}{27}$.

So, simplify the numerator: 12 ÷ 3 = 4

Then simplify the denominator: 27 ÷ 3 = 9

STEP 3: Use the results from step 2 to form the new fraction.

The numerator from step 2 is 4.

The denominator is 9.

So, the new fraction is $\frac{4}{9}$.

Mixed Numbers

Mixed numbers are those that contain a whole number and a fraction.

 Convert the mixed numbers back to fractions first. Then find the lowest common denominator of the fractions in order to solve the problem.

Problem:

$3\frac{1}{3} - 2\frac{1}{2} = ?$

A. $\frac{1}{3}$

B. $\frac{9}{3}$

C. $\dfrac{5}{6}$

D. $1\dfrac{1}{2}$

The correct answer is C.

Our problem was: $3\dfrac{1}{3} - 2\dfrac{1}{2} = ?$

STEP 1: Convert the first mixed number to an integer plus a fraction.

$3\dfrac{1}{3} =$

$3 + \dfrac{1}{3}$

STEP 2: Then multiply the integer by a fraction whose numerator and denominator are the same as the denominator of the existing fraction.

$3 + \dfrac{1}{3} =$

$\left(3 \times \dfrac{3}{3}\right) + \dfrac{1}{3} =$

$\dfrac{9}{3} + \dfrac{1}{3}$

STEP 3: Add the two fractions to get your new fraction.

$\dfrac{9}{3} + \dfrac{1}{3} = \dfrac{10}{3}$

Then convert the second mixed number to a fraction, using the same steps that we have just completed for the first mixed number.

$2\dfrac{1}{2} =$

$2 + \dfrac{1}{2} =$

$$\left(2 \times \frac{2}{2}\right) + \frac{1}{2} =$$

$$\frac{4}{2} + \frac{1}{2} = \frac{5}{2}$$

Now that you have converted both mixed numbers to fractions, find the lowest common denominator and subtract to solve.

$$\frac{10}{3} - \frac{5}{2} =$$

$$\left(\frac{10}{3} \times \frac{2}{2}\right) - \left(\frac{5}{2} \times \frac{3}{3}\right) =$$

$$\frac{20}{6} - \frac{15}{6} =$$

$$\frac{5}{6}$$

PEMDAS – Order of Operations

The phrase "order of operations" means that you need to know which mathematical operation to do first when you are faced with longer problems.

Remember the acronym PEMDAS. "PEMDAS" means that you have to do the mathematical operations in this order:

First: Do operations inside **P**arentheses

Second: Do operations with **E**xponents

Third: Perform **M**ultiplication and **D**ivision (from left to right)

Last: Do **A**ddition and **S**ubtraction (from left to right)

Some students prefer to remember the order or operations by using the memorable phrase:

 Please Excuse My Dear Aunt Sally

So, refer to the rules above and attempt the example problems that follow.

Problem 1:

−6 × 3 − 4 ÷ 2 = ? −18−2
                    −20

A. −20

B. −18

C. −2

D. 4

The correct answer is A.

There are no parentheses or exponents in this problem, so we need to direct our attention to the multiplication and division first.

Our problem was: −6 × 3 − 4 ÷ 2 = ?

When you see a problem like this one, you need to do the multiplication and division from left to right.

This means that you take the number to the left of the multiplication or division symbol and multiply or divide that number on the left by the number on the right of the symbol.

So, in our problem we need to multiply −6 by 3 and then divide 4 by 2.

You can see the order of operations more clearly if you put in parentheses to group the numbers together.

−6 × 3 − 4 ÷ 2 =

(−6 × 3) − (4 ÷ 2) =

−18 − 2 =

−20

Now try a problem that has parenthesis, exponents, multiplication, division, addition, and subtraction.

Problem 2:

$$\frac{5 \times (7-4)^2 + 3 \times 8}{5 - 6 \div (4-1)} = ?$$

A. −23

B. 23

C. $\dfrac{23}{1/3}$

D. 128

The correct answer is B.

For this type of problem, do the operations inside the **parentheses** first.

$$\frac{5 \times (7-4)^2 + 3 \times 8}{5 - 6 \div (4-1)} =$$

$$\frac{5 \times (3)^2 + 3 \times 8}{5 - 6 \div 3}$$

Then do the operation on the **exponent**.

$$\frac{5 \times (3)^2 + 3 \times 8}{5 - 6 \div 3} =$$

$$\frac{5 \times (3 \times 3) + 3 \times 8}{5 - 6 \div 3}$$

$$\frac{5 \times 9 + 3 \times 8}{5 - 6 \div 3}$$

Then do the **multiplication** and **division**.

$$\frac{5 \times 9 + 3 \times 8}{5 - 6 \div 3} =$$

$$\frac{(5 \times 9) + (3 \times 8)}{5 - (6 \div 3)} =$$

$$\frac{45+24}{5-2}$$

Then do the **addition** and **subtraction**.

$$\frac{45+24}{5-2} = \frac{69}{3}$$

In this case, we can then simplify the fraction since both the numerator and denominator are divisible by 3.

$$\frac{69}{3} = 69 \div 3 = 23$$

Percentages and Decimals

You will have to calculate percentages and decimals on the exam, as well as use percentages and decimals to solve other types of math problems or to create equations.

 Percentages can be expressed by using the symbol %. They can also be expressed as fractions or decimals.

In general, there are three ways to express percentages.

TYPE 1: Percentages as fractions

Percentages can always be expressed as the number over one hundred.

So 45% = $^{45}/_{100}$

TYPE 2: Percentages as simplified fractions

Percentages can also be expressed as simplified fractions.

In order to simplify the fraction, you have to find the largest number that will go into both the numerator and denominator.

In the case of 45%, the fraction is $^{45}/_{100}$, and the numerator and denominator are both divisible by 5.

To simplify the numerator: 45 ÷ 5 = 9.

To simplify the denominator: 100 ÷ 5 = 20.

This results in the simplified fraction of $9/20$.

TYPE 3: Percentages as decimals

Percentages can also be expressed as decimals.

45% = $45/100$ = 45 ÷ 100 = 0.45

You may have to use these concepts in order to solve a practical problem, like the one that follows.

Problem:

Consider a class which has n students. In this class, $t\%$ of the students subscribe to digital TV packages.

Which of the following equations represents the number of students who do not subscribe to any digital TV package?

A. $100(n - t)$

B. $(100\% - t\%) \times n$

C. $(100\% - t\%) \div n$

D. $(1 - t)n$

The correct answer is B.

If $t\%$ subscribe to digital TV packages, then $100\% - t\%$ do not subscribe.

In other words, since a percentage is any given number out of 100%, the percentage of students who do not subscribe is represented by this equation:

$(100\% - t\%)$

This equation is then multiplied by the total number of students (n) in order to determine the number of students who do not subscribe to digital TV packages.

$(100\% - t\%) \times n$

Proportions

A proportion is an equation with a ratio on each side.

In other words, a proportion is a statement that two ratios are equal.

$^3/_4 = {^6/_8}$ is an example of a proportion.

We will look at ratios in more depth in the subsequent section.

 Proportions often involve simplifying fractions, which we have learned how to do in a previous section.

Proportions can be expressed as fractions, as in the following problem.

Problem:

Find the value of x that solves the following proportion: $^3/_6 = {^x/_{14}}$

A. 3

B. 6

C. 7

D. 9

The correct answer is C.

STEP 1: You can <u>simplify</u> the first fraction because both the numerator and denominator are divisible by 3.

$^3/_6 \div {^3/_3} = {^1/_2}$

STEP 2: Then divide the denominator of the second fraction ($^x/_{14}$) by the denominator of the simplified fraction ($^1/_2$) from above.

14 ÷ 2 = 7

STEP 3: Now, multiply the number from step 2 by the numerator of the fraction we calculated in step 1 in order to get your result.

1 × 7 = 7

You can check your answer as follows:

$3/6 = 7/14$

$3/6 \div 3/3 = 1/2$

$7/14 \div 7/7 = 1/2$

Ratios

Ratios take a group of people or things and divide them into two parts.

For example, if your teacher tells you that each day you should spend two hours studying math for every hour that you spend studying English, you get the ratio 2:1.

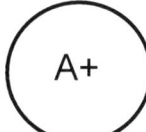

Ratios can be expressed as fractions. Ratios can also be expressed by using the colon. For example, a ratio of 2 to 100 can be expressed as $2/100$ or 2:100.

The number before the colon expresses one subset of the total amount of items.

The number after the colon expresses a different subset of the total.

In other words, when the number before the colon and the number after the colon are added together, we have the total amount of items.

Problem:

In a shipment of 100 mp3 players, 1% are faulty.

What is the ratio of non-faulty mp3 players to faulty mp3 players?

A. 1:100

B. 99:100

C. 1:99

D. 99:1

The correct answer is D.

This problem is asking for the quantity of non-faulty mp3 players to the quantity of faulty mp3 players.

Therefore, you must put the quantity of non-faulty mp3 players before the colon in the ratio.

In this problem, 1% of the players are faulty.

1% × 100 = 1 faulty player in every 100 players

100 − 1 = 99 non-faulty players

As explained above, the number before the colon and the number after the colon can be added together to get the total quantity.

So, the ratio is 99:1.

Setting Up Basic Equations

You will see problems on the test that ask you to make mathematical equations from basic information.

To set up an equation, read the problem carefully and then express the facts in terms of an algebraic equation.

These types of questions are often practical problems that involve buying or selling merchandise.

Problem 1:

A company purchases cell phones at a cost of x and sells the cell phones at four times the cost.

Which of the following represents the profit made on each cell phone?

A. x

B. $3x$

C. $4x$

D. $3 - x$

The correct answer is B.

The sales price of each cell phone is four times the cost.

The cost is expressed as x, so the sales price is $4x$.

The difference between the sales price of each cell phone and the cost of each cell phone is the profit.

REMEMBER: Sales Price − Cost = Profit

In this problem, the sales price is 4x and the cost is x.

4x − x = Profit

3x = Profit

Problem 2:

An internet provider sells internet packages based on monthly rates. The price for the internet service depends on the speed of the internet connection.

The chart that follows indicates the prices of the various internet packages.

Price in dollars (P)	10	20	30	40
Gigabyte speed (s)	2	4	6	8

Which equation represents the prices of these internet packages?

A. $P = (s - 5) \times 5$ $P = (2-5) \cdot 5 = 3 \cdot 5 = 15$

B. $P = (s + 5) \times 5$ $P = (2+5) \times 5 = 7 \times 5 = 35$

C. $P = 5 \div s$ $P = 5 \div 2 = 2.5$

D. $P = s \times 5$ $P = 2 \cdot 5 = 10$

The correct answer is D.

The price of the internet connection is always 5 times the speed.

10 = 2 × 5

20 = 4 × 5

30 = 6 × 5

40 = 8 × 5

So, the price of the internet connection (represented by variable P) equals the speed (represented by variable s) times 5.

P = s × 5

Working with Averages

Basic averages are calculated by taking the total of a data set for a group and then dividing this total by the number of people in the group.

For example, have a look at the following problem.

Three people are trying to lose weight. The first person has lost 7 pounds, the second person has lost 10 pounds, and the third person has lost 16 pounds. What is the average weight loss for this group?

STEP 1: Add all of the individual amounts together to get a total for the group.

7 + 10 + 16 = 33

STEP 2: Divide the total from step 1 by the number of people in the group.

33 ÷ 3 = 11

So, the average weight loss is 11 pounds.

However, problems with averages on the PERT Test will quite often be more difficult than the one provided above.

Problems that you see on the exam might involve an average that was calculated in error. Find the total of the data set by reversing the erroneous operation. Then divide the total by the correct number of items in order to find the correct average.

Other types of problems will give you averages for two distinct members of a group, like male and female students in a class, and then ask you to calculate the average for the entire group.

For advanced problems on averages, multiply each average by the number of people in each group. Then add the totals for each group together and divide by the total number of people.

Problem:

120 students took a math test. The 60 female students in the class had an average score of 95, while the 60 male students in the class had an average of 90. What is the average test score for all 120 students in the class?

A. 75

B. 92.5

C. 93

D. 93.5

The correct answer is B.

STEP 1: You need to find the total points for all the females by multiplying their average by the number of female students. Then do the same to find the total points for all the males.

Females: 60 × 95 = 5700

Males: 60 × 90 = 5400

STEP 2: Then add these two amounts together to get the total for the group.

5700 + 5400 = 11,100

STEP 3: Then divide by the total number of students in the class to get your solution.

11,100 ÷ 120 = 92.5

So, the correct average is 92.5

Algebra concepts and formulas:

The algebra and college algebra parts of the exam cover:

- the FOIL method and other operations with polynomials
- factoring polynomial expressions
- fractions containing rational and radical expressions
- inequalities
- laws of exponents
- multiple solutions
- practical problems
- solving problems by substitution and elimination
- solving problems for an unknown variable
- square roots
- systems of equations

You may also see some coordinate geometry problems on the test.

That is because you need to use algebraic concepts to solve coordinate geometry problems.

Coordinate geometry is covered in the next section of the study guide.

The FOIL Method and Working with Polynomials

Polynomials are algebraic expressions that contain integers, variables, and variables which are raised to whole-number positive exponents.

You will certainly see problems involving polynomials on the PERT Test. Be sure that you know these concepts well.

Multiplying Polynomials Using the FOIL Method:

The use of the FOIL method is one of the most important things you will need to know in order to answer many of the algebra questions on the test.

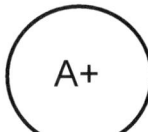

You will see many problems in this format on the test: $(x + y)(x + y)$. Use the FOIL method to solve these problems, multiplying the terms in the parentheses in this order: First – Outside – Inside – Last

Look at the example algebra question below on the FOIL method. Note that there are several other problems covering this skill in the practice problems that follow this part of the study guide.

Problem:

$(3x - 2y)^2 = ?$

A. $9x^2 + 4y^2$

B. $9x^2 - 6xy^2 + 4y^2$

C. $9x^2 - 12xy + 4y^2$

D. $9x^2 + 12xy + 4y^2$

The correct answer is C.

When you see algebra questions like this one, use the FOIL method.

Study the solution below, which highlights the order to carry out the operations on the terms.

$(3x - 2y)^2 = (3x - 2y)(3x - 2y)$

FIRST: The first terms in each set of parentheses are $3x$ and $3x$: **($3x$** $- 2y)($**$3x$** $- 2y)$

$3x \times 3x = 9x^2$

OUTSIDE: The terms on the outside are 3x and −2y: (**3x** − 2y)(3x − **2y**)

3x × −2y = −6xy

INSIDE: The terms on the inside are −2y and 3x: (3x − **2y**)(**3x** − 2y)

−2y × 3x = −6xy

LAST: The last terms in each set are −2y and −2y: (3x − **2y**)(3x − **2y**)

−2y × −2y = 4y^2

All of these individual results are put together for your final answer to the question.

9x^2 − 6xy − 6xy + 4y^2 =

9x^2 − 12xy + 4y^2

Dividing Polynomials Using Long Division:

You may also need to perform long division on polynomials on the exam.

> You can think of long division of the polynomial as reversing the FOIL operation. In other words, your result will generally be in one of the following formats: (x + y) or (x − y)

Problem:

(x^2 − x − 6) ÷ (x − 3) = ?

A. 2x

B. x − 2

C. x − 2

D. x + 2

The correct answer is D.

In order to solve this type of problem, you must do long division of the polynomial.

Remember that you are subtracting the terms when you perform each part of the long division, so you need to be careful with negatives.

$$\begin{array}{r}x+2\\ x-3\overline{)x^2-x-6}\\ \underline{x^2-3x}\\ 2x-6\\ \underline{2x-6}\\ 0\end{array}$$

Substituting Values in Polynomial Expressions:

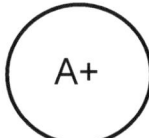

You may be asked to calculate the value of an expression by substituting its values. To solve these problems, put in the values for x and y and multiply. Then do the addition and subtraction.

Problem:

What is the value of the expression $4x^2 + 2xy - y^2$ when $x = 2$ and $y = -2$?

A. 4

B. 6

C. 8

D. 12

The correct answer is A.

$4x^2 + 2xy - y^2 =$

$(4 \times 2^2) + (2 \times 2 \times -2) - (-2^2) =$

$(4 \times 2 \times 2) + (2 \times 2 \times -2) - (-2 \times -2) =$

$(4 \times 4) + (2 \times -4) - (4) =$

$16 + (-8) - 4 =$

$16 - 12 = 4$

Operations on Polynomials Containing Three Terms:

You might also see problems on the exam in which you have to carry out operations on polynomial expressions that have more than two terms.

 If you see polynomial expressions that have more than two terms inside each set of parentheses, remember to use the distributive property of multiplication to solve the problem.

To solve these types of problems, you will also need to understand basic exponent laws.

We will look at exponents in more detail in the "Law of Exponents" section.

Problem:

Perform the operation: $(5ab - 6a)(3ab^3 - 4b^2 - 3a)$

A. $15a^2b^4 - 20ab^3 - 15a^2b - 18a^2b^3 - 24ab^2 - 18a^2$

B. $15a^2b^4 - 20ab^3 - 15a^2b - 18a^2b^3 + 24ab^2 + 18a^2$

C. $15a^2b^4 - 20ab^3 - 15a^2b - 18a^2b^3 - 24ab^2 + 18a^2$

D. $15ab^4 - 20ab^3 - 15a^2b - 18a^2b^3 + 24ab^2 + 18a^2$

The correct answer is B.

STEP 1: Apply the distributive property of multiplication by multiplying the first term in the first set of parentheses by all of the terms inside the second pair of parentheses.

Then multiply the second term from the first set of parentheses by all of the terms inside the second set of parentheses.

$(5ab - 6a)(3ab^3 - 4b^2 - 3a) =$

$(5ab \times 3ab^3) + (5ab \times -4b^2) + (5ab \times -3a) + (-6a \times 3ab^3) + (-6a \times -4b^2) + (-6a \times -3a)$

STEP 2: Add up the individual products in order to solve the problem.

$(5ab \times 3ab^3) + (5ab \times -4b^2) + (5ab \times -3a) + (-6a \times 3ab^3) + (-6a \times -4b^2) + (-6a \times -3a) =$

$15a^2b^4 - 20ab^3 - 15a^2b - 18a^2b^3 + 24ab^2 + 18a^2$

Factoring Polynomials

Factoring means that you have to break down a polynomial into smaller parts.

You can factor by looking for integers or variables that are common to all of the terms of the equation.

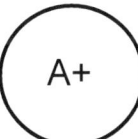 In order to factor an equation, you must figure out what variables are common to each term of the equation.

Basic Factoring:

Some problems will involve placing a term in front of a set of parentheses, as in the following example.

Problem:

Factor the following: $2xy - 6x^2y + 4x^2y^2$

A. $2xy(1 + 3x - 2xy)$

B. $2xy(1 - 3x + 2xy)$

C. $2xy(1 + 3x + 2xy)$

D. $2xy(1 - 3x - 2xy)$

The correct answer is B.

Looking at this equation, we can see that each term contains x. We can also see that each term contains y.

So, first factor out xy.

$2xy - 6x^2y + 4x^2y^2 =$

$xy(2 - 6x + 4xy)$

Then, think about integers. We can see that all of the terms inside the parentheses are divisible by 2.

Now let's factor out the 2. To do this, we divide each term inside the parentheses by 2.

$xy(2 - 6x + 4xy) =$

$2xy(1 - 3x + 2xy)$

Factoring – Advanced Problems:

You will also see problems like the one below that include more than one polynomial.

These types of problems often involve multiplying or dividing fractions that contain rational expressions.

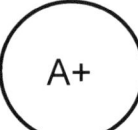

In order to factor problems containing more than one polynomial, you will need to find the factors of the terms inside each set of parentheses.

We will look at this concept again in the section entitled "Fractions Containing Rational Expressions."

Problem:

Factor the following. Then simplify. $\dfrac{x^2+5x+6}{x^2+6x+8} \times \dfrac{x^2+4x}{x^2+8x+15}$

A. $\dfrac{5}{x+5}$

B. $\dfrac{x}{x+5}$

C. $\dfrac{x+3}{x+4}$

D. $\dfrac{x+4}{x+3}$

The correct answer is B.

$\dfrac{x^2+5x+6}{x^2+6x+8} \times \dfrac{x^2+4x}{x^2+8x+15} = ?$

For this type of problem, first you need to find the factors of the numerators and denominators of each fraction.

When there are only addition signs in the rational expression, the factors will be in the following format:

(+)(+)

If there is a negative sign, then the factors will be in this format:

(+)(−)

You have to find the factors of the terms containing x or y variables, as well as the factors of the integers or other constants.

It is usually best to start with finding the factors of the final integer in each polynomial expression.

STEP 1: The numerator of the first fraction is $x^2 + 5x + 6$, so the final integer is 6.

The factors of 6 are:

1 × 6 = 6

2 × 3 = 6

Add these factors together to discover what integer you need to use in front of the second term of the expression.

1 + 6 = 7

2 + 3 = 5

2 and 3 satisfy both parts of the equation.

Therefore, the factors of $x^2 + 5x + 6$ are $(x + 2)(x + 3)$.

Now factor the other parts of the problem.

STEP 2: The denominator of the first fraction is $x^2 + 6x + 8$, so the final integer is 8.

The factors of 8 are:

1 × 8 = 8

2 × 4 = 8

Then add these factors together to find the integer to use in front of the second term of the expression.

1 + 8 = 9

2 + 4 = 6

Therefore, the factors of $x^2 + 6x + 8$ are $(x+2)(x+4)$.

STEP 3: The numerator of the second fraction is $x^2 + 4x$, so there is no final integer.

Because x is common to both terms of the expression, the factor will be in this format:

$x(x +)$

Therefore, in order to factor $x^2 + 4x$, we express it as $x(x+4)$.

STEP 4: The denominator of the second fraction is $x^2 + 8x + 15$, so the final integer is 15.

The factors of 15 are:

1 × 15 = 15

3 × 5 = 15

Add these factors together to find the integer to use in front of the second term of the expression.

1 + 15 = 16

3 + 5 = 8

Therefore, the factors of $x^2 + 8x + 15$ are $(x+3)(x+5)$.

A good shortcut for this type of problem is to remind yourself that it is a problem about factoring, so the factors you find in step 1 will probably be common to other parts of the expression.

In other words, we discovered in step 1 that the factors of $x^2 + 5x + 6$ are $(x+2)$ and $(x+3)$.

So, when you are factoring out the other parts of the problem, start with $(x+2)$ and $(x+3)$.

Now that we have completed all of the four steps above, we can set out our problem with the factors we discovered in each step.

We can see the factors of each fraction more clearly as follows:

$$\frac{x^2 + 5x + 16}{x^2 + 6x + 18} = \frac{(x+2)(x+3)}{(x+2)(x+4)} \qquad \frac{x^2 + 4x}{x^2 + 8x + 15} = \frac{x(x+4)}{(x+3)(x+5)}$$

The problem should be set up as follows after you have found the factors:

$$\frac{x^2+5x+6}{x^2+6x+8} \times \frac{x^2+4x}{x^2+8x+15} =$$

$$\frac{(x+2)(x+3)}{(x+2)(x+4)} \times \frac{x(x+4)}{(x+3)(x+5)}$$

Then you need to simplify by removing the common factors.

Remove $(x + 2)$ from the first fraction.

$$\frac{(x+2)(x+3)}{(x+2)(x+4)} \times \frac{x(x+4)}{(x+3)(x+5)} =$$

$$\frac{(x+3)}{(x+4)} \times \frac{x(x+4)}{(x+3)(x+5)}$$

Once you have simplified each fraction as much as possible, perform the operation indicated.

In this problem, we are multiplying. So, we can express the two factored-out fractions as one fraction and then remove the other common terms.

$$\frac{(x+3)}{(x+4)} \times \frac{x(x+4)}{(x+3)(x+5)} =$$

$$\frac{(x+3)(x+4)x}{(x+4)(x+3)(x+5)}$$

You can remove $(x + 3)$ from the above fraction since it is in both the numerator and denominator.

$$\frac{(x+3)(x+4)x}{(x+4)(x+3)(x+5)} =$$

$$\frac{(x+4)x}{(x+4)(x+5)}$$

We can further simplify by removing $(x + 4)$.

$$\frac{(x+4)x}{(x+4)(x+5)} =$$

$$\frac{x}{(x+5)}$$

So, our final answer is $\frac{x}{x+5}$

Factoring to Find Possible Values of a Variable:

You may see problems on the exam that give you a polynomial expression and ask you to determine possible values for the variables in the expression.

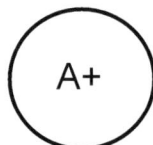

> **A+** If you are asked to find values for variables such as x or y in a math problem, substitute zero for one variable. Then substitute zero for the other variable in order to solve the problem.

Problem:

What are two possible values of x for the following equation? $x^2 + 6x + 8 = 0$

A. 1 and 2

B. 2 and 4

C. 6 and 8

D. −2 and −4

The correct answer is D.

STEP 1: Factor the equation.

$x^2 + 6x + 8 = 0$

$(x + 2)(x + 4) = 0$

STEP 2: Now substitute 0 for x in the first pair of parentheses.

$(0 + 2)(x + 4) = 0$

$2(x + 4) = 0$

$2x + 8 = 0$

$2x + 8 − 8 = 0 − 8$

2x = – 8

2x ÷ 2 = – 8 ÷ 2

x = –4

STEP 3: Then substitute 0 for x in the second pair of parentheses.

(x + 2)(x + 4) = 0

(x + 2)(0 + 4) = 0

(x + 2)4 = 0

4x + 8 = 0

4x + 8 – 8 = 0 – 8

4x = –8

4x ÷ 4 = –8 ÷ 4

x = –2

Fractions Containing Fractions

On the college algebra part of the exam, you will see fractions that have fractions in their numerators or denominators.

| A+ | When you see fractions containing fractions, remember to treat the denominator as the division sign. Then invert the second fraction and multiply. |

Problem:

$$\frac{x + \frac{1}{5}}{\frac{1}{x}} = ?$$

A. $x^2 + 5$

B. $\dfrac{x^3}{5}$

C. $x^2 + \dfrac{x}{5}$

D. $\dfrac{x + \dfrac{1}{5}}{x}$

The correct answer is C.

As stated above, the fraction can also be expressed as division.

$$\dfrac{x + \dfrac{1}{5}}{\dfrac{1}{x}} = \left(x + \dfrac{1}{5}\right) \div \dfrac{1}{x}$$

Then invert the second fraction and multiply the fractions as usual.

In this case $\dfrac{1}{x}$ becomes $\dfrac{x}{1}$ when inverted, which is then simplified to x.

$\left(x + \dfrac{1}{5}\right) \div \dfrac{1}{x} =$

$\left(x + \dfrac{1}{5}\right) \times x =$

$x^2 + \dfrac{x}{5}$

Fractions Containing Radicals

You may see fractions that contain radicals in the numerator or denominator.

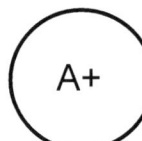

A+ — If your problem has a fraction that contains a radical in its numerator or denominator, you need to eliminate the radical by multiplying both sides of the equation by the radical.

Problem:

If $\dfrac{30}{\sqrt{x^2 - 75}} = 6$, then $x = ?$

A. 100

B. 30

C. 25

D. 10

The correct answer is D.

Eliminate the radical in the denominator by multiplying both sides of the equation by the radical.

$$\frac{30}{\sqrt{x^2 - 75}} = 6$$

$$\frac{30}{\sqrt{x^2 - 75}} \times \sqrt{x^2 - 75} = 6 \times \sqrt{x^2 - 75}$$

$$30 = 6\sqrt{x^2 - 75}$$

Then eliminate the integer in front of the radical.

$$30 = 6\sqrt{x^2 - 75}$$

$$30 \div 6 = \left(6\sqrt{x^2 - 75}\right) \div 6$$

$$5 = \sqrt{x^2 - 75}$$

Then eliminate the radical by squaring both sides of the equation, and solve for *x*.

$$5 = \sqrt{x^2 - 75}$$

$$5^2 = \left(\sqrt{x^2 - 75}\right)^2$$

$$25 = x^2 - 75$$

$$25 + 75 = x^2 - 75 + 75$$

$$100 = x^2$$

$$x = 10$$

Fractions Containing Rational Expressions

On the algebra and college-level math parts of the exam, you may see fractions that contain rational expressions.

Rational expressions are math problems that contain algebraic terms.

Adding and Subtracting Fractions Containing Rational Expressions:

You may have to add or subtract two fractions that contain rational expressions.

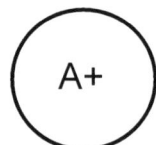

> **A+** To add or subtract two fractions that contain rational expressions, you need to calculate the lowest common denominator, just like you would for any other problem with fractions.

Problem :

$$\frac{x^5}{x^2 - 6x} + \frac{5}{x} = ?$$

A. $\dfrac{4 + x^6}{x^2 - 3x}$

B. $\dfrac{4x^2 - 16x}{x^7}$

C. $\dfrac{x^5 + 5x + 30}{x^2 - 6x}$

D. $\dfrac{x^5 + 5x - 30}{x^2 - 6x}$

The correct answer is D.

Find the lowest common denominator. Since x is common to both denominators, we can convert the denominator of the second fraction to the LCD by multiplying by $(x - 6)$.

$$\frac{x^5}{x^2 - 6x} + \frac{5}{x} =$$

$$\frac{x^5}{x^2 - 6x} + \left(\frac{5}{x} \times \frac{x - 6}{x - 6}\right) =$$

$$\frac{x^5}{x^2-6x} + \frac{5x-30}{x^2-6x} =$$

$$\frac{x^5+5x-30}{x^2-6x}$$

Multiplying Fractions Containing Rational Expressions:

The following problem asks you to multiply two fractions, both of which contain rational expressions.

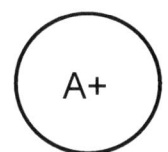

A+ | To multiply fractions containing rational expressions, multiply the numerator of the first fraction by the numerator of the second fraction to get the new numerator. Then multiply the denominators.

Problem:

$$\frac{2x^3}{5} \times \frac{4}{x^2} = ?$$

A. $\dfrac{8x}{5}$

B. $\dfrac{5}{8x}$

C. $\dfrac{8}{5}$

D. $8x$

The correct answer is A.

Multiply the numerator of the first fraction by the numerator of the second fraction. Then multiply the denominators.

$$\frac{2x^3}{5} \times \frac{4}{x^2} = \frac{8x^3}{5x^2}$$

Then factor the numerator and denominator.

As stated previously, we will discuss operations on exponents in more depth in the "Laws of Exponents" section of the study guide.

$$\frac{8x^3}{5x^2} = \frac{8x(x^2)}{5(x^2)}$$

Then we can cancel out x^2 to solve the problem.

$$\frac{8x(x^2)}{5(x^2)} = \frac{8x}{5}$$

Dividing Fractions Containing Rational Expressions:

You may also be asked to divide two fractions, both of which contain rational expressions.

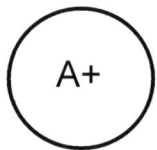

A+ — In order to divide fractions that contain rational expressions, invert the second fraction and multiply. Then cancel out any common factors. Be sure to cancel out completely.

Problem:

$$\frac{6x+6}{x^2} \div \frac{3x+3}{x^3} = ?$$

A. $2x$

B. $6x$

C. $18x^3$

D. $\frac{3x+3}{x}$

The correct answer is A.

The first step in solving the problem is to invert and multiply by the second fraction.

$$\frac{6x+6}{x^2} \div \frac{3x+3}{x^3} =$$

$$\frac{6x+6}{x^2} \times \frac{x^3}{3x+3} =$$

$$\frac{x^3(6x+6)}{x^2(3x+3)}$$

Then factor the numerator and denominator. $(x + 1)$ is common to both the numerator and the denominator, so we can factor that out.

$$\frac{x^3(6x+6)}{x^2(3x+3)} =$$

$$\frac{x^3 6(x+1)}{x^2 3(x+1)}$$

Now cancel out the $(x + 1)$.

$$\frac{x^3 6(x+1)}{x^2 3(x+1)} =$$

$$\frac{x^3 6}{x^2 3} =$$

$$\frac{6x^3}{3x^2}$$

Now factor out x^2 and cancel it out.

$$\frac{6x^3}{3x^2} =$$

$$\frac{6x \times x^2}{3x^2} =$$

$$\frac{6x}{3}$$

The numerator and denominator share the factor of 3, so cancel out further in order to get your final result.

$$\frac{6x}{3} =$$

$$\frac{3 \times 2 \times x}{3} =$$

$2x$

Inequalities

Inequality problems will have a less than or greater than sign. There may be more than one equation in a single inequality problem on the PERT exam.

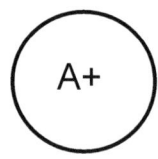

> **A+** When solving inequality problems, isolate integers before dealing with any fractions. Also remember that if you multiply an inequality by a negative number, you have to reverse the direction of the less than or greater than sign.

Problem 1:

$40 - \frac{3x}{5} \geq 10$, then $x \leq$?

A. 15

B. 30

C. 40

D. 50

The correct answer is D.

Deal with the whole numbers on each side of the equation first.

$$40 - \frac{3x}{5} \geq 10$$

$$(40 - 40) - \frac{3x}{5} \geq 10 - 40$$

$$-\frac{3x}{5} \geq -30$$

Then deal with the fraction.

$$-\frac{3x}{5} \geq -30$$

$$\left(5 \times -\frac{3x}{5}\right) \geq -30 \times 5$$

$-3x \geq -30 \times 5$

$-3x \geq -150$

Then deal with the remaining whole numbers.

$-3x \geq -150$

$-3x \div 3 \geq -150 \div 3$

$-x \geq -150 \div 3$

$-x \geq -50$

Then deal with the negative number.

$-x \geq -50$

$-x + 50 \geq -50 + 50$

$-x + 50 \geq 0$

Finally, isolate the unknown variable as a positive number.

$-x + 50 \geq 0$

$-x + x + 50 \geq 0 + x$

$50 \geq x$

$x \leq 50$

Problem 2:

Inequalities may also be expressed in practical problems like the one below.

In the equations below, x represents the cost of one online game and y represents the cost of one movie ticket.

If x − 2 > 5 and y = x − 2, then the cost of 2 discounted movie tickets is greater than which one of the following?

A. $x - 2$

B. $x - 5$

C. $y + 5$

D. 10

The correct answer is D.

For problems like this, look to see if both of the equations have any variables or terms in common.

In this problem, both equations contain $x - 2$.

The cost of one movie ticket is represented by y, and y is equal to $x - 2$.

Therefore, we can substitute values from one equation to another.

$x - 2 > 5$

$y > 5$

If two tickets are being purchased, we need to solve for $2y$.

$y \times 2 > 5 \times 2$

$2y > 10$

Laws of Exponents

You will need to know exponent laws very well for the examination.

You will see questions on the exam that involve adding and subtracting exponents.

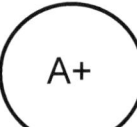

> **A+** When the base numbers are the same and you need to multiply, you add the exponents. When the base numbers are the same and you need to divide, you subtract the exponents.

We can prove the above concepts as shown below.

For multiplication with a variable:

$x^4 \times x^2 = x^6$

$x^6 = x \times x \times x \times x \times x \times x$

For multiplication with an integer:

$2^3 \times 2^2 = 2^5$

$8 \times 4 = 32$

$2^5 = 2 \times 2 \times 2 \times 2 \times 2 = 32$

For division with a variable:

$y^5 \div y^3 = y^2$

$y^2 = y \times y$

For division with an integer:

$2^3 \div 2^2 = 2^1 = 2$

$8 \div 4 = 2$

Do not get confused when you are asked to add or subtract the variables or integers themselves.

Example with a variable: $x^2 + x^2 = 2x^2$

Example with integers: $2^3 + 2^2 = 8 + 4 = 12$

Now try the problems that follow.

Adding exponents:

Problem:

$11^5 \times 11^3 = ?$

A. 11^8

B. 11^{15}

C. 22^8

D. 121^8

The correct answer is A.

The base number in this example is 11.

So, we add the exponents: 5 + 3 = 8

That is:

$11^5 \times 11^3 =$

$11^{(5+3)} =$

11^8

Subtracting exponents:

Problem:

$10^6 \div 10^4 = ?$

A. 10^{24}

B. 10^2

C. 20^{24}

D. 20^2

The correct answer is B.

The base number in this example is 10.

So, we subtract the exponents: $6 - 4 = 2$

$10^6 \div 10^4 =$

$10^{(6-4)} =$

10^2

Multiple Solutions

You will see questions on the exam that give you an equation and then ask you how many solutions there are for the equation provided.

A+ — You will need to consider both positive and negative numbers as potential solutions.

Problem 1:

How many solutions exist for the following equation?

$x^2 + 8 = 0$

A. 0

B. 1

C. 2

D. 4

The correct answer is A.

Remember that any real number squared will always equal a positive number.

Since 8 is added to the first value x^2, the result will always be 8 or greater.

In other words, since x^2 is always a positive number, the result of the equation would never be 0.

So, there are zero solutions for this equation.

Problem 2:

How many solutions exist for the following equation?

$x^2 - 9 = 0$

A. 0

B. 1

C. 2

D. 4

The correct answer is C.

Any real number squared will always equal a positive number.

Since 9 is subtracted from x^2, x^2 needs to be equal to 9.

Both 3 and −3 solve the equation. So, there are two solutions for this equation.

Practical Problems

Several questions on the PERT Test will ask you to solve practical problems.

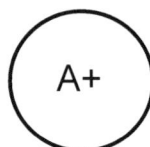

> A+ | Practical problems may involve calculating a discount on an item in a store. Other common practical problems involve calculations with exam scores or other data for a class of students.

Now have a look at another type of practical problem, which involves knowledge of basic equations.

We will look at basic equations in more depth in the "Setting Up Basic Equations" section of this study guide.

For some basic equation problems, you will see two equations which have the same two variables, like J and T in the problem below.

Problem:

A company sells jeans and T-shirts. J represents jeans and T represents T-shirts in the equations below.

$2J + T = \$50$

$J + 2T = \$40$

Sarah buys one pair of jeans and one T-shirt. How much does she pay for her entire purchase?

A. $10

B. $20

C. $30

D. $70

The correct answer is C.

In order to solve the problem, take the second equation and isolate J on one side of the equation. By doing this, you define variable J in terms of variable T.

$J + 2T = \$40$

$J + 2T - 2T = \$40 - 2T$

$J = \$40 - 2T$

Now substitute $\$40 - 2T$ for variable J in the first equation to solve for variable T.

$2J + T = 50$

$2(40 - 2T) + T = 50$

$80 - 4T + T = 50$

$80 - 3T = 50$

$80 - 3T + 3T = 50 + 3T$

$80 = 50 + 3T$

$80 - 50 = 50 - 50 + 3T$

$30 = 3T$

$30 \div 3 = 3T \div 3$

$10 = T$

So, now that we know that a T-shirt costs $10, we can substitute this value in one of the equations in order to find the value for the jeans, which is variable J.

$2J + T = 50$

$2J + 10 = 50$

$2J + 10 - 10 = 50 - 10$

$2J = 40$

$2J \div 2 = 40 \div 2$

$J = 20$

Now solve for Sarah's purchase. If she purchased one pair of jeans and one T-shirt, then she paid:

$\$10 + \$20 = \$30$

Solving by Elimination

When you have to solve a problem by elimination, you will see two equations as in the following question.

A+ — In order to solve by elimination, you need to subtract the second equation from the first equation.

Problem:

Solve the following by elimination.

$x + 4y = 30$

$2x + 2y = 36$

A. $x = 2$ and $y = 7$

B. $x = 4$ and $y = 14$

C. $x = 14$ and $y = 4$

D. $x = 16$ and $y = 2$

The correct answer is C.

Look at the x term of the second equation, which is $2x$.

In order to eliminate the x variable, we need to multiply the first equation by 2 and then subtract the second equation from this result.

$x + 4y = 30$

$(2 \times x) + (2 \times 4y) = (30 \times 2)$

$2x + 8y = 60$

Now subtract the two equations.

$$\begin{array}{r} 2x + 8y = 60 \\ -(2x + 2y = 36) \\ \hline 6y = 24 \end{array}$$

Then solve for y.

$6y = 24$

$6y \div 6 = 24 \div 6$

$y = 4$

Using our first equation $x + 4y = 30$, substitute the value of 4 for y to solve for x.

$x + 4y = 30$

$x + (4 \times 4) = 30$

$x + 16 = 30$

$x + 16 - 16 = 30 - 16$

$x = 14$

Solving for an Unknown Variable

You will certainly see problems involving solving equations for an unknown variable on the exam.

> **A+** Perform the multiplication on the items in parentheses first. Then eliminate the integers and solve for x.

Problem:

If $3x - 2(x + 5) = -8$, then $x = ?$

A. 1

B. 2

C. 3

D. 5

The correct answer is B.

To solve this type of problem, do multiplication on the items in parentheses first.

$3x - 2(x + 5) = -8$

49

© COPYRIGHT 2008-2014. Academic Success Media DBA www.college-placement-test.com
This material may not be copied or reproduced in any form.

$3x - 2x - 10 = -8$

Then deal with the integers by putting them on one side of the equation.

$3x - 2x - 10 + 10 = -8 + 10$

$3x - 2x = 2$

Then solve for x.

$3x - 2x = 2$

$1x = 2$

$x = 2$

Square Roots, Cube Roots, and Other Radicals

Square roots and cube roots are sometimes referred to as radicals.

You will need to know how to perform the operations of multiplication and division on square and cube roots.

You will also see problems that involve rationalizing and factoring square and cube roots.

Factoring radicals:

Factoring radicals requires the same concepts as factoring integers or polynomial expressions.

You have to find the factors of the numbers inside the square root symbols.

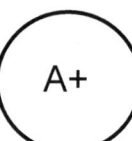

> **A+** In order to factor a radical, you need to find the squared factors of the number inside the radical sign. For example:
> $\sqrt{128} = \sqrt{64 \times 2} = \sqrt{8 \times 8 \times 2} = 8\sqrt{2}$

Problem 1:

Which of the answers below is equal to the following radical expression? $\sqrt{45}$

A. $1 \div 45$

B. $5\sqrt{9}$

C. $9\sqrt{5}$

D. $3\sqrt{5}$

The correct answer is D.

For square root problems like this one, you need to remember certain mathematical principles.

First, remember to factor the number inside the square root sign.

The factors of 45 are:

1 × 45 = 45

3 × 15 = 45

5 × 9 = 45

Then look to see if any of these factors have square roots that are whole numbers.

In this case, the only factor whose square root is a whole number is 9.

Now find the square root of 9.

$\sqrt{9} = 3$

Finally, you need to put this number at the front of the square root sign and put the other factor inside the square root sign in order to solve the problem.

$\sqrt{45} =$

$\sqrt{9 \times 5} =$

$\sqrt{3 \times 3 \times 5} =$

$3\sqrt{5}$

Problem 2:

You may see advanced problems on radicals involving other operations, such as addition or subtraction.

$\sqrt{32} + 2\sqrt{72} + 3\sqrt{18} = ?$

A. $2\sqrt{16} + 2\sqrt{36} + 3\sqrt{9}$

B. $5\sqrt{122}$

C. $6\sqrt{122}$

D. $25\sqrt{2}$

The correct answer is D.

First you need to find the squared factors of the amounts inside the radical signs.

In this problem, 16, 36, and 9 are squared factors of each radical because $16 = 4^2$, $36 = 6^2$, and $9 = 3^2$.

$\sqrt{32} + 2\sqrt{72} + 3\sqrt{18} =$

$\sqrt{2 \times 16} + 2\sqrt{2 \times 36} + 3\sqrt{2 \times 9}$

Then expand the amounts inside the radicals for the factors and simplify.

$\sqrt{2 \times 16} + 2\sqrt{2 \times 36} + 3\sqrt{2 \times 9} =$

$\sqrt{2 \times (4 \times 4)} + 2\sqrt{2 \times (6 \times 6)} + 3\sqrt{2 \times (3 \times 3)} =$

$4\sqrt{2} + (2 \times 6)\sqrt{2} + (3 \times 3)\sqrt{2} =$

$4\sqrt{2} + 12\sqrt{2} + 9\sqrt{2} =$

$25\sqrt{2}$

Multiplication of radicals:

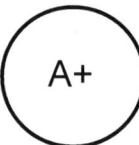

A+ — To multiply radicals, multiply the numbers inside the square root signs. Then put this result inside a square root symbol for your answer. For example: $\sqrt{x} \times \sqrt{y} = \sqrt{xy}$

Problem:

$\sqrt{6} \times \sqrt{5} = ?$

A. $\sqrt{30}$

B. $\sqrt{11}$

C. $6\sqrt{5}$

D. $5\sqrt{6}$

The correct answer is A.

Multiply the numbers inside the square root signs first.

6 × 5 = 30

Then put this result inside a square root symbol for your answer.

$\sqrt{30}$

Rationalizing radicals:

You may see problems on the exam that ask you to rationalize a number or to express a radical number as a rational number.

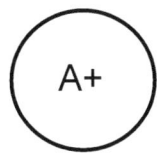

> **A+** Perform the necessary mathematical operations in order to remove the square root symbol. This normally involves factoring in order to find square or cube roots.

Problem:

Express as a rational number: $\sqrt[3]{\dfrac{64}{125}}$

A. $1/5$

B. $4/5$

C. $5/4$

D. $125/64$

The correct answer is B.

In this problem, you have to find the cube roots of the numerator and denominator in order to eliminate the radical.

Remember that the cube root is the number which satisfies the equation when multiplied by itself two times.

$$\sqrt[3]{\frac{64}{125}} = \sqrt[3]{\frac{4 \times 4 \times 4}{5 \times 5 \times 5}} = \frac{4}{5}$$

Systems of Equations

For these problems, you will see two equations, both of which will contain *x* and *y*. In one equation, *x* and *y* will be added. In the other equation, *x* and *y* will be multiplied.

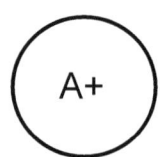

> **A+** In order to solve systems of equations, look at the equation that contains multiplication first. Then find the factors of the product in the equation to solve the problem.

Problem:

What ordered pair is a solution to the following system of equations?

$x + y = 9$

$xy = 20$

A. (2, 7)

B. (2, 10)

C. (3, 6)

D. (4, 5)

The correct answer is D.

For questions on systems of equations like this one, you should look at the multiplication equation first.

Ask yourself, what are the factors of 20? We know that 20 is the product of the following:

$1 \times 20 = 20$

$2 \times 10 = 20$

$4 \times 5 = 20$

Now add each of the two factors together to solve the first equation.

1 + 20 = 21

2 + 10 = 12

4 + 5 = 9

(4, 5) solves both equations, so it is the correct answer.

Coordinate geometry concepts and formulas:

On the PERT Exam, you will need to know coordinate geometry for problems like:

- Calculating the slope of the line
- Determining the slope-intercept formula for given points on a graph
- Calculating the distance between two points on a graph
- Determining the midpoint between two points
- Finding *x* and *y* intercepts

Many students ask why they need to know coordinate geometry for the PERT exam, since the test is designed to cover basic mathematical and algebraic concepts.

The answer is that coordinate geometry is included on the PERT because you need to understand how to use algebraic principles in order to solve coordinate geometry problems.

So, be sure that you understand the coordinate geometry concepts in this section of the study guide before you take your exam.

Distance formula

The distance formula is used to calculate the linear distance between two points on a two-dimensional graph.

The two points are represented by the coordinates (x_1, y_1) and (x_2, y_2).

A+ The distance formula is as follows: $d = \sqrt{(x_2 - x_1)^2 + (y_2 - y_1)^2}$

Problem:

What is the distance between (1,0) and (5,4)?

A. 4

B. 5

C. 16

D. $\sqrt{32}$

The correct answer is D.

Substitute values into the distance formula from the facts stated in the problem.

$d = \sqrt{(x_2 - x_1)^2 + (y_2 - y_1)^2}$

$d = \sqrt{(5 - 1)^2 + (4 - 0)^2}$

$d = \sqrt{4^2 + 4^2}$

$d = \sqrt{16 + 16}$

$d = \sqrt{32}$

Midpoints

You may be asked to calculate the midpoint of two points on a graph.

Remember that you divide the sum of the two points by 2 because the midpoint is the halfway mark between the two points on the line.

The two points are represented by the coordinates (x_1, y_1) and (x_2, y_2).

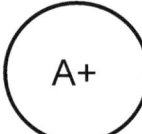

> **A+** The midpoints of two points on a two-dimensional graph are calculated by using the midpoint formula: $(x_1 + x_2) \div 2$, $(y_1 + y_2) \div 2$

You might see problems like the following one on the exam:

Find the coordinates (x, y) of the midpoint of the line segment on a graph that connects the points (−4, 8) and (2, −6).

However, you may also need to use the midpoint formula in practical problems, like the one that follows.

Problem:

Consider two stores in a town. The first store is a grocery store. The second is a pizza place where customers collect their pizzas after they order them online.

The grocery store is represented by the coordinates (−4, 2) and the pizza place is represented by the coordinates (2, −4).

If the grocery store and the pizza place are connected by a line segment, what is the midpoint of this line?

A. (1, 1)

B. (−1, −1)

C. (2, 2)

D. (−2, −2)

The correct answer is B.

Remember that to find midpoints, you need to use these formulas:

midpoint $x = (x_1 + x_2) \div 2$

midpoint $y = (y_1 + y_2) \div 2$

First, find the midpoint of the *x* coordinates for (**−4**, 2) and (**2**,−4).

midpoint $x = (x_1 + x_2) \div 2$

midpoint $x = (-4 + 2) \div 2$

midpoint $x = -2 \div 2$

midpoint $x = -1$

Then find the midpoint of the *y* coordinates for (−4, **2**) and (2,**−4**).

midpoint $y = (y_1 + y_2) \div 2$

midpoint $y = (2 + -4) \div 2$

midpoint $y = -2 \div 2$

midpoint $y = -1$

So, the midpoint is (−1, −1)

Slope and Slope-Intercept

Calculating slope is one of the most important skills that you will need for coordinate geometry problems on the exam.

To put it in simple language, slope is the measurement of how steep a straight line on a graph is.

Slope will be negative when the line slants upwards to the left.

On the other hand, slope will be positive when the line slants upwards to the right.

The two points are represented by the coordinates (x_1, y_1) and (x_2, y_2).

Slope is represented by variable *m*.

We can calculate slope by using the slope formula.

> **A+** The slope formula is as follows: $m = \dfrac{y_2 - y_1}{x_2 - x_1}$

You will sometimes be given a set of points, and then told where the line crosses the y axis. In that case, you will also need what is known as the slope-intercept formula.

In the slope-intercept formula, *m* is the slope, *b* is the *y* intercept (the point at which the line crosses the *y* axis), and *x* and *y* are points on the graph.

> **A+** Here is the slope-intercept formula: $y = mx + b$

Problem:

Marta runs up and down a hill near her house. The measurements of the hill can be placed on a two dimensional linear graph on which *x* = 5 and *y* = 165. If the line crosses the *y* axis at 15, what is the slope of this hill?

A. 10

B. 20

C. 30

D. 36

The correct answer is C.

Substitute the values into the formula.

y = *mx* + *b*

165 = *m*5 + 15

165 − 15 = *m*5 + 15 − 15

150 = *m*5

150 ÷ 5 = *m*5 ÷ 5

30 = m

x and y intercepts

You may also be asked to calculate x and y intercepts in plane geometry problems.

The x intercept is the point at which a line crosses the x axis of a graph.

In order for the line to cross the x axis, y must be equal to zero at that particular point of the graph.

On the other hand, the y intercept is the point at which the line crosses the y axis.

So, in order for the line to cross the y axis, x must be equal to zero at that particular point of the graph.

> **A+** For questions about x and y intercepts, substitute 0 for y in the equation provided. Then substitute 0 for x to solve the problem.

Problem:

Find the x and y intercepts of the following equation: $x^2 + 4y^2 = 64$

A. (8, 0) and (0, 4)

B. (0, 8) and (4, 0)

C. (4, 0) and (0, 8)

D. (0, 4) and (8, 0)

The correct answer is A.

Remember to substitute 0 for y in order to find the x intercept.

$x^2 + 4y^2 = 64$

$x^2 + (4 \times 0) = 64$

$x^2 + 0 = 64$

$x^2 = 64$

$x = 8$

hen substitute 0 for x in order to find the y intercept.

$x^2 + 4y^2 = 64$

$(0 \times 0) + 4y^2 = 64$

$0 + 4y^2 = 64$

$4y^2 \div 4 = 64 \div 4$

$y^2 = 16$

$y = 4$

So, the y intercept is (0, 4) and the x intercept is (8, 0).

PART 2 – PERT MATH PRACTICE TESTS

PERT Math Practice Test 1:

1) Two people are going to give money to a foundation for a project. Person A will provide one-half of the money. Person B will donate one-eighth of the money. What fraction represents the unfunded portion of the project?

   A) 1/16

   B) 1/8

   C) 1/4

   D) 3/8

2) A hockey team had 50 games this season and lost 20 percent of them. How many games did the team win?

   A) 8

   B) 10

   C) 20

   D) 40

3) Carmen wanted to find the average of the five tests she has taken this semester. However, she erroneously divided the total points from the five tests by 4, which gave her a result of 90. What is the correct average of her five tests?

   A) 64

   B) 72

   C) 80

   D) 90

4) Beth took a test that had 60 questions. She got 10% of her answers wrong. How many questions did she answer correctly?

   A) 6

   B) 10

   C) 50

   D) 54

5) Professor Smith uses a system of extra-credit points for his class. Extra-credit points can be offset against the points lost on an exam due to incorrect responses.

David answered 18 questions incorrectly on the exam and lost 36 points. He then earned 25 extra credit points. By how much was his exam score ultimately lowered?

A) −11

B) 11

C) 18

D) 25

6) A group of friends are trying to lose weight. Person A lost $14^{3}/_{4}$ pounds. Person B lost $20^{1}/_{5}$ pounds. Person C lost 36.35 pounds. What is the total weight loss for the group?

A) 70.475

B) 71.05

C) 71.15

D) 71.30

7) A job is shared by 4 workers, A, B, C, and D. Worker A does $^{1}/_{6}$ of the total hours. Worker B does $^{1}/_{3}$ of the total hours. Worker C does $^{1}/_{6}$ of the total hours. What fraction represents the remaining hours allocated to person D?

A) $^{1}/_{8}$

B) $^{3}/_{8}$

C) $^{1}/_{6}$

D) $^{1}/_{3}$

8) The university bookstore is having a sale. Course books can be purchased for $40 each, or 5 books can be purchased for a total of $150. How much would a student save on each book if he or she purchased 5 books?

A) 5

B) 10

C) 50

D) 90

9) One hundred students took an English test. The 55 female students in the class had an average score of 87, while the 45 male students in the class had an average of 80. What is the average test score for all 100 students in the class?

A) 82.00

B) 83.15

C) 83.50

D) 83.85

10) Mary needs to get $650 in donations. So far, she has obtained 80% of the money she needs. How much money does she still need?

A) $8.19

B) $13.00

C) $32.50

D) $130.00

11) The graph of $y = 8 \div (x - 4)$ is shown below.

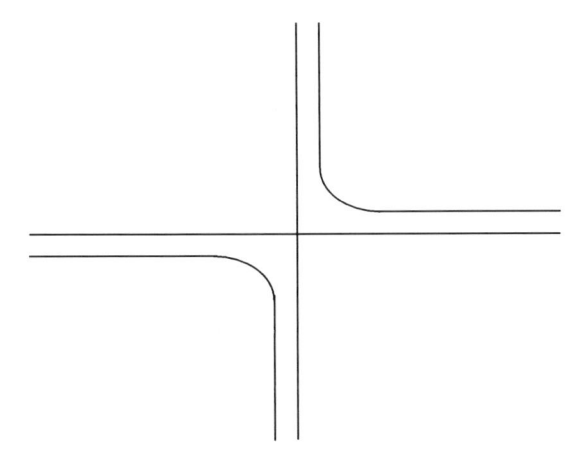

Which of the following is the best representation of $8 \div |(x - 4)|$?

A.

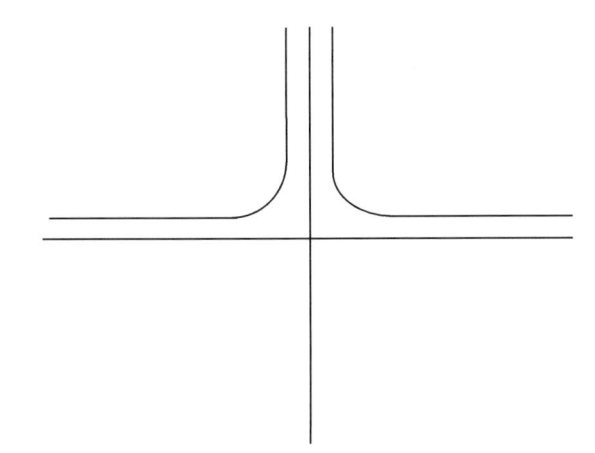

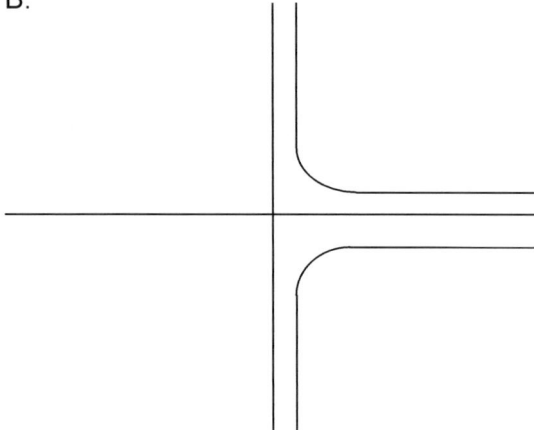

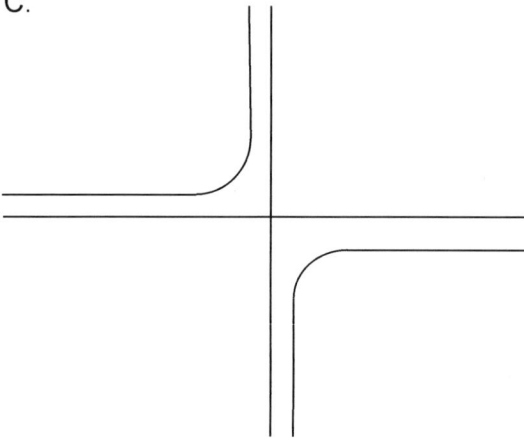

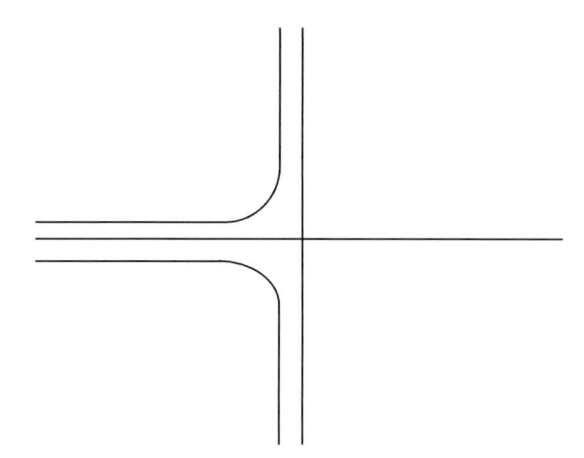

B.

C.

D.

12) Which of the following is the graph of the solution set of –3x > 6?

A.

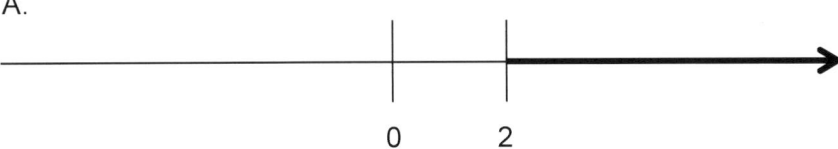

```
————————|——|—————————————→
         0  2
```

B.

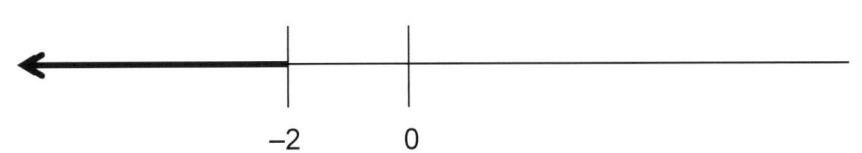

```
←—————————|——|———————————————
         –2  0
```

C.

```
—————|————|————|————————→
    –4    0    4
```

D.

```
|—————————|—————————|————→
–6        0         6
```

13) $(x^2 – 4) \div (x + 2) = ?$

A) $x + 2$

B) $x – 2$

C) $x + 2x^2$

D) $x – x^2$

14) If $5x – 2(x + 3) = 0$, then $x = ?$

A) –2

B) –1

C) 1

D) 2

15) Simplify the following equation: $(x + 3y)^2$

A) $2(x – 3y)$

B) $2x + 6y$

C) $x^2 + 6xy - 9y^2$

D) $x^2 + 6xy + 9y^2$

16) $(x + 3y)(x - y) = ?$

   A) $x^2 + 2xy - 3y^2$

   B) $2x + 2xy - 2y$

   C) $x^2 - 2xy + 3y^2$

   D) $2x - 2xy + 2y$

17) What is the value of the expression $6x^2 - xy + y^2$ when $x = 5$ and $y = -1$?

   A) 36

   B) 144

   C) 146

   D) 156

18) Two people are going to work on a job. The first person will be paid $7.25 per hour. The second person will be paid $10.50 per hour. If A represents the number of hours the first person will work, and B represents the number of hours the second person will work, what equation represents the total cost of the wages for this job?

   A) 17.75AB

   B) 17.75 ÷ AB

   C) AB ÷ 17.75

   D) (7.25A + 10.50B)

19) $x^2 + xy - y = 41$ and $x = 5$. What is the value of y?

   A) 2.6

   B) 4

   C) 6

   D) –4

20) $20 - \dfrac{3x}{4} \geq 17$, then $x \leq ?$

   A) –12

   B) –4

C) –3

D) 4

21) Factor: $18x^2 - 2x$

   A) $2x(9x-1)$

   B) $9x(2x-1)$

   C) $2x(9x-x)$

   D) $9x(2x-x)$

22) Simplify the following: $(5x^2 + 3x - 4) - (6x^2 - 5x + 8)$

   A) $-x^2 - 2x + 4$

   B) $-x^2 - 2x - 12$

   C) $-x^2 + 8x + 4$

   D) $-x^2 + 8x - 12$

23) $(x - 4)(3x + 2) = ?$

   A) $3x^2 - 10x - 8$

   B) $3x^2 - 10x + 8$

   C) $3x^2 + 14x - 8$

   D) $3x^2 + 14x + 8$

24) Simplify: $\sqrt{7} + 2\sqrt{7}$

   A) 14

   B) $3\sqrt{7}$

   C) $2\sqrt{14}$

   D) $3\sqrt{14}$

25) Factor the following: $x^2 + x - 20$

   A) $x(x - 1) - 20$

   B) $(x - 5)(x - 4)$

   C) $(x - 5)(x + 4)$

   D) $(x + 5)(x - 4)$

26) $(x - 4y)^2 = ?$

    A) $x^2 + 16y^2$

    B) $x^2 - 8xy - 16y^2$

    C) $x^2 - 8xy + 16y^2$

    D) $x^2 + 8xy - 16y^2$

27) If $4x - 3(x + 2) = -3$, then $x = ?$

    A) 9

    B) 3

    C) 1

    D) −3

28) $(x^2 - x - 12) \div (x - 4) = ?$

    A) $(x + 3)$

    B) $(x - 3)$

    C) $(-x + 3)$

    D) $(-x - 3)$

29) Mark's final grade for a course is based on the grades from two tests, A and B. Test A counts toward 35% of his final grade. Test B counts toward 65% of his final grade. What equation is used to calculate Mark's final grade for this course?

    A) .65A + .35B

    B) .35A + .65B

    C) (.35A + .65B) ÷ 2

    D) A + B

30) What is the value of the expression $2x^2 + 3xy - y^2$ when $x = 3$ and $y = -3$?

    A) −18

    B) 0

    C) 18

    D) 36

PERT Math Practice Test 2:

1) $\sqrt{2} \times \sqrt{3} = ?$

   A) 6

   B) $\sqrt{5}$

   C) $\sqrt{6}$

   D) $\sqrt{18}$

2) Simplify: $(x - 2y)(2x - y)$

   A) $2x^2 - 3xy + 2y^2$

   B) $2x^2 + 3xy + 2y^2$

   C) $2x^2 - 5xy + 2y^2$

   D) $2x^2 - 5xy - 2y^2$

3) $20 + \dfrac{x}{4} \geq 22$, then $x \geq ?$

   A) –8

   B) –2

   C) 0

   D) 8

4) State the *x* and *y* intercepts that fall on the straight line represented by the following equation:

   $y = x + 6$

   A) (–6,0) and (0,6)

   B) (0,6) and (0,–6)

   C) (6,0) and (0,–6)

   D) (0,–6) and (6,0)

5) $(5x + 7y) + (3x - 9y) = ?$

   A) $2x - 2y$

   B) $2x + 16y$

   C) $8x + 2y$

   D) $8x - 2y$

6) If $5x - 4(x + 2) = -2$, then $x = $?

   A) 0

   B) 8

   C) 6

   D) –8

7) Simplify: $(x - y)(x + y)$

   A) x^2

   B) $x^2 - 2xy - y^2$

   C) $x^2 + 2xy - y^2$

   D) $x^2 - y^2$

8) $\sqrt{8} \times \sqrt{2} = $?

   A) $8\sqrt{2}$

   B) $2\sqrt{8}$

   C) $\sqrt{4}$

   D) 4

9) Factor the following: $2xy - 8x^2y + 6y^2x^2$

   A) $2(xy - 4x^2y + 3x^2y^2)$

   B) $2xy(-4x + 3xy)$

   C) $2xy(1 - 4x + 3xy)$

   D) $2xy(1 + 4x - 3xy)$

10) $(x + 3) - (4 - x) = $?

    A) –7

    B) –1

    C) $2x - 1$

    D) $2x + 1$

11) If $x - 1 > 0$ and $y = x - 1$, then $y > $?

    A) x

    B) $x + 1$

C) x – 1

D) 0

12) Find the coordinates (x, y) of the midpoint of the line segment on a graph that connects the points (–5, 3) and (3, –5).

A) (–1,–1)

B) (–1,1)

C) (1,–1)

D) (1,1)

13) The price of socks is $2 per pair and the price of shoes is $25 per pair. Anna went shopping for socks and shoes, and she paid $85 in total. In this purchase, she bought 3 pairs of shoes. How many pairs of socks did she buy?

A) 2

B) 3

C) 5

D) 8

14) Consider a two-dimensional linear graph where x = 3 and y = 14. The line crosses the y axis at 5. What is the slope of this line?

A) 2.2

B) 3.0

C) 6.33

D) –2.2

15) If $5 + 5(3\sqrt{x} + 4) = 55$, then $\sqrt{x}$ = ?

A) –4

B) –2

C) 2

D) 4

16) Factor the following equation: $6xy - 12x^2y - 24y^2x^2$

A) $6(xy - 2x^2y - 4x^2y^2)$

B) $xy(6 - 12x - 24xy)$

C) $6xy(-2x - 4xy)$

D) $6xy(1 - 2x - 4xy)$

17) If x – 5 < 0 and y < x + 10, then y < ?

A) 5

B) –5

C) 0

D) 15

18) Find the x and y intercepts of the following equation: $4x^2 + 9y^2 = 36$

A) (3,0) and (0,2)

B) (0,2) and (0,3)

C) (2,0) and (3,0)

D) (2,0) and (0,3)

19) Find the midpoint between the following coordinates: (2, 2) and (4, –6)

A) (3,4)

B) (3,–4)

C) (3,2)

D) (3,–2)

20) If $4 + 3(2\sqrt{x} - 3) = 25$, then x = ?

A) –5

B) –25

C) 5

D) 25

21) The Smith family is having lunch in a diner. They buy hot dogs and hamburgers to eat. The hot dogs cost $2.50 each, and the hamburgers cost $4 each. They buy 3 hamburgers. They also buy hot dogs. The total value of their purchase is $22. How many hot dogs did they buy?

A) 3

B) 4

C) 5

D) 6

22) Simplify: $(x + 5) - (x^2 - 2x)$

A) $-x - x^2 + 5$

B) $-x + x^2 - 5$

C) $x - x^2 + 5$

D) $3x - x^2 + 5$

23) $(-3x^2 + 7x + 2) - (x^2 - 5) = ?$

A) $-2x^2 + 7x - 3$

B) $-2x^2 + 7x + 7$

C) $-4x^2 + 7x - 3$

D) $-4x^2 + 7x + 7$

24) $\dfrac{x^2 + 10x + 16}{x^2 + 11x + 18} \times \dfrac{x^2 + 9x}{x^2 + 17x + 72} = ?$

A) $\dfrac{9}{x + 9}$

B) $\dfrac{x}{x + 9}$

C) $\dfrac{x^2}{x^2 + 17x}$

D) $\dfrac{x + 1}{x + 8}$

25) $\sqrt{5b - 4} = 4$ What is the value of b?

A) 0

B) $5/4$

C) 4

D) $4/5$

26) $\dfrac{5z-5}{z} \div \dfrac{6z-6}{5z^2} = ?$

A) $\dfrac{6}{25z}$

B) $\dfrac{30z^2+30}{5z^3}$

C) $\dfrac{6z^2-6z}{25z^2-25z}$

D) $\dfrac{25z}{6}$

27) If $c = \dfrac{a}{1-b}$, then $b = ?$

A) $\dfrac{c}{a}$

B) $\dfrac{a}{c} - 1$

C) $-\dfrac{a}{c} + 1$

D) $c - ca$

28) $\sqrt{14x^5} \times \sqrt{6x^3} = ?$

A) $\sqrt{20x^{15}}$

B) $\sqrt{84x^{15}}$

C) $2x^4\sqrt{21}$

D) $2x^8\sqrt{21}$

29) $8ab^2(3ab^4 + 2b) = ?$

A) $11a^2b^6 + 10ab^3$

B) $24a^2b^8 + 16ab^3$

C) $48ab^6 + 32ab^2$

D) $24a^2b^6 + 16ab^3$

30) Perform the operation and express as one fraction: $\dfrac{5}{12x} + \dfrac{4}{10x^2} = ?$

A) $\dfrac{9}{22x^3}$

B) $\dfrac{48x}{50x^2}$

C) $\dfrac{29}{12x}$

D) $\dfrac{25x + 24}{60x^2}$

PERT Math Practice Test 3:

1) In the standard (x, y) plane, what is the distance between $(3\sqrt{3}, -1)$ and $(6\sqrt{3}, 2)$?

   A) 6

   B) 27

   C) 36

   D) $3\sqrt{3} + 1$

2) Perform the operation: $\sqrt{5}(\sqrt{20} - \sqrt{5})$

   A) $5\sqrt{15}$

   B) $\sqrt{45}$

   C) 25

   D) 5

3) $8^7 \times 8^3 = ?$

   A) 8^4

   B) 8^{10}

   C) 8^{21}

   D) 64^{10}

4) Solve by elimination.

   $x + 5y = 24$

   $8x + 2y = 40$

   A) (4, 4)

   B) (−4, 4)

   C) (40, 4)

   D) (4, 38)

5) Perform the operation: $(4x - 3)(5x^2 + 12x + 11) = ?$

   A) $20x^3 + 33x^2 + 80x - 33$

   B) $20x^3 + 33x^2 + 80x + 33$

   C) $20x^3 + 33x^2 + 8x - 33$

   D) $20x^3 + 33x^2 - 8x - 33$

6) $\sqrt{6x^3}\sqrt{24x^5} = ?$

A) $12\sqrt{x^{15}}$

B) $\sqrt{30x^8}$

C) $12x^4$

D) $144x^4$

7) $\sqrt{18} + 3\sqrt{32} + 5\sqrt{8} = ?$

A) $17\sqrt{2}$

B) $25\sqrt{2}$

C) $8\sqrt{58}$

D) $15\sqrt{58}$

8) What equation represents the slope-intercept formula for the following data?

Through (4, 5); $m = -3/5$

A) $y = -\dfrac{3}{5}x + 5$

B) $y = -\dfrac{12}{5}x - 5$

C) $y = -\dfrac{3}{5}x - \dfrac{37}{5}$

D) $y = -\dfrac{3}{5}x + \dfrac{37}{5}$

9) For all $a \neq b$, $\dfrac{\frac{5a}{b}}{\frac{2a}{a-b}} = ?$

A) $\dfrac{10a^2}{ab - b^2}$

B) $\dfrac{a-b}{2b}$

C) $\dfrac{5a-5}{2}$

D) $\dfrac{5a-5b}{2b}$

10) Perform the operation and express as one fraction: $\dfrac{1}{a+1}+\dfrac{1}{a}$

A) $\dfrac{2}{2a+1}$

B) $\dfrac{a+1}{a}$

C) $\dfrac{a^2+a}{2a+1}$

D) $\dfrac{2a+1}{a^2+a}$

11) $\dfrac{\sqrt{48}}{3}+\dfrac{5\sqrt{5}}{6}=?$

A) $\dfrac{4\sqrt{3}+5\sqrt{5}}{6}$

B) $\dfrac{8\sqrt{3}+5\sqrt{5}}{6}$

C) $\dfrac{\sqrt{48}+5\sqrt{5}}{9}$

D) $\dfrac{6\sqrt{48}+5\sqrt{5}}{18}$

12) For all $x \neq 0$ and $y \neq 0$, $\dfrac{4x}{1/xy} = ?$

   A) $\dfrac{4x}{xy}$

   B) $\dfrac{xy}{4x}$

   C) $\dfrac{4x}{y}$

   D) $4x^2y$

13) $10a^2b^3c \div 2ab^2c^2 = ?$

   A) $5c \div ab$
   B) $5a \div bc$
   C) $5ab \div c$
   D) $5ac \div b$

14) If x and y are positive integers, the expression $\dfrac{1}{\sqrt{x} - \sqrt{y}}$ is equivalent to which of the following?

   A) $\sqrt{x} - y$

   B) $\sqrt{x} + y$

   C) $\dfrac{\sqrt{x} - y}{1}$

   D) $\dfrac{\sqrt{x} + \sqrt{y}}{x - y}$

15) $(2 + \sqrt{6})^2 = ?$

   A) 8

   B) $8 + 2\sqrt{6}$

C) $8 + 4\sqrt{6}$

D) $10 + 4\sqrt{6}$

16) $\sqrt[3]{5} \times \sqrt[3]{7} = ?$

   A) $\sqrt[3]{13}$

   B) $\sqrt[6]{13}$

   C) $\sqrt[9]{13}$

   D) $\sqrt[3]{35}$

17) What is the value of $\dfrac{x-3}{2-x}$ when $x = 1$?

   A) 2

   B) –2

   C) $-1/2$

   D) $-1/2$

18) The term PPM, pulses per minute, is used to determine how many heartbeats an individual has every 60 seconds. In order to calculate PPM, the pulse is taken for ten seconds, represented by variable P. What equation is used to calculate PPM?

   A) PPM ÷ 60

   B) PPM ÷ 10

   C) P6

   D) P10

19) Medical authorities have recommended that an individual's ideal PPM is 60. What equation is used to calculate by how much a person's PPM exceeds the ideal PPM?

   A) 60 + PPM

   B) 60 – PPM

   C) PPM + 60

   D) PPM – 60

20) A runner of a 100 mile endurance race ran at a speed of 5 miles per hour for the first 80 miles of the race and *x* miles per hour for the last 20 miles of the race. What equation represents the runner's average speed for the entire race?

A) $100 \div [(80 \div 5) + (20 \div x)]$

B) $100 \times [(80 \div 5) + (20 \div x)]$

C) $100 \div [(80 \times 5) + (20 \times x)]$

D) $100 \times [(80 \times 5) + (20 \times x)]$

21) $3^4 \times 3^3 = ?$

A) 9^{12}

B) 9^7

C) 6^{12}

D) 3^7

22) The number of bottles of soda that a soft drink factory can produce during *D* number of days using production method A is represented by the following equation:

$D^5 + 12{,}000$

Alternatively, the number of bottles of soda that can be produced using production method B is represented by this equation:

$D \times 10{,}000$

What is the largest number of bottles of soda that can be produced by the factory during a 10 day period?

A) 10,000

B) 12,000

C) 100,000

D) 112,000

23) $5^8 \div 5^2 = ?$

A) 25^6

B) 25^4

C) 5^6

D) 5^4

24) A driver travels at 60 miles per hour for two and a half hours before her car fails to start at a service station. She has to wait two hours while the car is repaired before she can continue driving. She then drives at 75 miles an hour for the remainder of her journey. She is traveling to Denver, and her journey is 240 miles in total. If she left home at 6:00 am, what time will she arrive in Denver?

   A) 9:30 am

   B) 11:30 am

   C) 11:42 am

   D) 11:50 am

25) Which one of the following is a solution to the following ordered pairs of equations?

   $y = -2x - 1$

   $y = x - 4$

   A) (0, 1)

   B) (1, -3)

   C) (4, 0)

   D) (1, 3)

26) At the beginning of a class, one-fourth of the students leave to attend band practice. Later, one half of the remaining students leave to go to PE. If there were 15 students remaining in the class at the end, how many students were in the class at the beginning?

   A) 40

   B) 45

   C) 50

   D) 55

27) Shania is entering a talent competition which has three events. The third event (C) counts three times as much as the second event (B), and the second event counts twice as much as the first event (A). What equation, expressed only in terms of variable A, can be used to calculate Shania's final score for the competition?

   A) 2A

   B) 3A

C) 6A

D) 9A

28) What ordered pair is a solution to the following system of equations?

x + y = 11

xy = 24

A) (3, 8)

B) (4, 6)

C) (2, 9)

D) (2, 12)

29) For all positive integers x and y, x – 6 < 0 and y < x + 12, then y < ?

A) 6

B) 12

C) 18

D) 24

30) Which of the following is the graph of the solution of 2 + y < –8?

A.

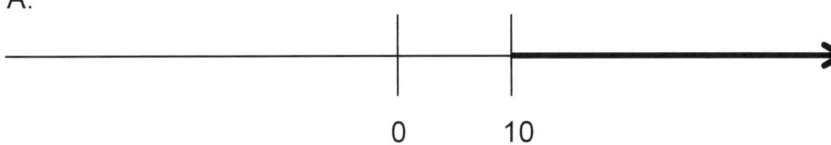

0   10

B.

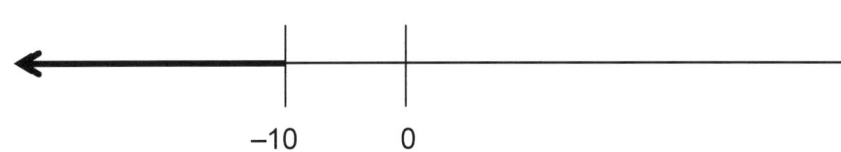

–10   0

C.

–10   0

D.

–16   0

ANSWERS AND SOLUTIONS TO THE PERT MATH PRACTICE TESTS

PERT Math Practice Test 1 – Answers:

1) The correct answer is D.

Two people are going to give money to a foundation for a project. Person A will provide one-half of the money. Person B will donate one-eighth of the money. What fraction represents the unfunded portion of the project?

The sum of all contributions must be equal to 100%, simplified to 1. Let's say that the variable U represents the unfunded portion of the project.

So the equation that represents this problem is $A + B + U = 1$

Substitute with the fractions that have been provided.

$$\frac{1}{2} + \frac{1}{8} + U = 1$$

For problems with fractions, you often have to find the lowest common denominator.

Finding the lowest common denominator means that you have to make all of the numbers on the bottoms of the fractions the same.

Remember that you need to find the common factors of the denominators in order to find the LCD.

We know that 2 and 4 are factors of 8.

So, the LCD for this question is 8 since the denominator of the first fraction is 2 and because 2 × 4 = 8.

So, we put the fractions into the LCD as follows:

$$\frac{1}{2} + \frac{1}{8} + U = 1$$

$$\left(\frac{1}{2} \times \frac{4}{4}\right) + \frac{1}{8} + U = 1$$

$$\frac{4}{8} + \frac{1}{8} + U = 1$$

$$\frac{5}{8} + U = 1$$

$$\frac{5}{8} - \frac{5}{8} + U = 1 - \frac{5}{8}$$

$$U = 1 - \frac{5}{8}$$

$$U = \frac{8}{8} - \frac{5}{8}$$

$$U = \frac{3}{8}$$

2) The correct answer is D.

A hockey team had 50 games this season and lost 20 percent of them. How many games did the team win?

For practical problems like this, you must first determine the percentage and formula that you need in order to solve the problem.

Then, you must do long multiplication to determine how many games the team won.

Be careful. The question tells you the percentage of games the team lost, not won.

So, first of all, we have to calculate the percentage of games won.

If the team lost 20 percent of the games, we know that the team won the remaining 80 percent.

Now do the long multiplication.

```
   50   games in total
× .80   percentage of games won (in decimal form)
 40.0   total games won
```

3) The correct answer is B.

Carmen wanted to find the average of the five tests she has taken this semester. However, she erroneously divided the total points from the five tests by 4, which gave her a result of 90. What is the correct average of her five tests?

First you need to find the total points that Carmen earned. You do this by taking Carmen's erroneous average times 4.

4 × 90 = 360

Then you need to divide the total points earned by the correct number of tests in order to get the correct average.

360 ÷ 5 = 72

4) The correct answer is D.

Beth took a test that had 60 questions. She got 10% of her answers wrong. How many questions did she answer correctly?

You must first determine the percentage of questions that Beth answered correctly.

We know that she got 10% of the answers wrong, so therefore the remaining 90% were correct.

Now we multiply the total number of questions by the percentage of correct answers.

60 × 90% = 54

5) The correct answer is B.

Professor Smith uses a system of extra-credit points for his class. Extra-credit points can be offset against the points lost on an exam due to incorrect responses. David answered 18 questions incorrectly on the exam and lost 36 points. He then earned 25 extra credit points. By how much was his exam score ultimately lowered?

Take the number of questions missed and add the extra credit points.

−36 + 25 = −11

Since the question is asking how much the score was lowered, you need to give the amount as a positive number.

6) The correct answer is D.

A group of friends are trying to lose weight. Person A lost $14^{3}/_{4}$ pounds. Person B lost $20^{1}/_{5}$ pounds. Person C lost 36.35 pounds. What is the total weight loss for the group?

Convert the fractions in the mixed numbers to decimals.

$^{3}/_{4}$ = 3 ÷ 4 = 0.75

$1/5 = 1 ÷ 5 = 0.20$

Then represent the mixed numbers as decimal numbers

Person 1: $14^3/_4 = 14.75$

Person 2: $20^1/_5 = 20.20$

Person 3: 36.35

Then add all three amounts together to find the total.

14.75 + 20.20 + 36.35 = 71.30

7) The correct answer is D.

A job is shared by 4 workers, A, B, C, and D. Worker A does $1/6$ of the total hours. Worker B does $1/3$ of the total hours. Worker C does $1/6$ of the total hours. What fraction represents the remaining hours allocated to person D?

The sum of the work from all four people must be equal to 100%, simplified to 1. In other words, they make up the total hours by working together.

A + B + C + D = 1

$1/6 + 1/3 + 1/6 + D = 1$

Now find the lowest common denominator of the fractions.

3 × 2 = 6, so the lowest common denominator is 6.

The fractions for Person A and Person C already have 6 in their denominators, so we only have to convert the fraction for Person B.

Convert the fraction as required.

$1/3 × 2/2 = 2/6$

Now add the fractions together.

$1/6 + 2/6 + 1/6 + D = 1$

$4/6 + D = 1$

$4/6 - 4/6 + D = 1 - 4/6$

D = 1 − $^4/_6$

D = $^2/_6$

D = $^1/_3$

8) The correct answer is B.

The university bookstore is having a sale. Course books can be purchased for $40 each, or 5 books can be purchased for a total of $150. How much would a student save on each book if he or she purchased 5 books?

First divide the total price for the multi-purchase by the number of items.

In this case, $150 ÷ 5 = $30 for each of the five books.

Then, subtract this amount from the original price to get your answer.

$40 − $30 = $10

Alternatively, you can use the method explained below.

Calculate the total price for the five books without the discount.

5 × $40 = $200

Then subtract the discounted price of $150 from the total.

$200 - $150 = $50

Then divide the total savings by the number of books to determine the savings on each book.

$50 total savings ÷ 5 books = $10 savings per book

9) The correct answer is D.

One hundred students took an English test. The 55 female students in the class had an average score of 87, while the 45 male students in the class had an average of 80. What is the average test score for all 100 students in the class?

First of all, you have to calculate the total amount of points earned by the entire class.

Multiply the female average by the amount of female students.

Total points for female students: 87 × 55 = 4785

Then multiply the male average by the amount of male students.

Total points for male students: 80 × 45 = 3600

Then add these two amounts together to find out the total points scored by the entire class.

Total points for entire class: 4785 + 3600 = 8385

When you have calculated the total amount of points for the entire class, you divide this by the total number of students in the class to get the class average.

8385 ÷ 100 = 83.85

10) The correct answer is D.

Mary needs to get $650 in donations. So far, she has obtained 80% of the money she needs. How much money does she still need?

We know that Mary has already gotten 80% of the money.

However, the question is asking how much money she still needs.

So, 100% – 80% = 20% and 20% = .20

Now do the multiplication.

650 × .20 = 130

11) The correct answer is A.

We know from the original graph in the question that when *x* is a positive number, then *y* will also be positive. This is represented by the curve in the upper right-hand quadrant of the graph.

We also know from the original graph in the question that when *x* is negative, *y* will also be negative. This is represented by the curve in the lower left-hand quadrant of the graph.

If we add the absolute value symbols to the problem, then | (*x* – 4) | will always result in a positive value for *y*.

Therefore, even when *x* is negative, *y* will be positive.

So, the curve originally represented in the lower left-hand quadrant of the graph must be shift into the upper left-hand quadrant.

12) The correct answer is B.

Isolate the unknown variable in order to solve the problem.

$-3x > 6$

$-3x \div 3 > 6 \div 3$

$-x > 2$

In order to solve the problem, we have to multiply each side of the equation by -1.

When we multiply both sides of an inequality by a negative number, we have to reverse the greater than symbol to a less than symbol (or if there is a less than symbol, we reverse it to a greater than symbol).

$-x \times -1 < 2 \times -1$

$x < -2$

In other words, if the isolated variable is negative as in this problem, you need to reverse the greater than symbol in order to make it the less than symbol.

$-x > 2$

$x < -2$

This is represented by line B.

13) The correct answer is B.

$(x^2 - 4) \div (x + 2) = ?$

First, look at the integers in the equation. In this problem the integers are -4 and 2.

We know that we have to divide -4 by 2 because the dividend is $(x + 2)$.

$-4 \div 2 = -2$

We also know that we have to divide x^2 by x, because these are the first terms in each set of parentheses.

$x^2 \div x = x$

Now combine the two parts.

$-2 + x = x - 2$

Check your result by doing long division of the polynomial.

```
              x – 2
      ┌─────────────
x + 2 )x²      – 4
       x² + 2x
       ─────────
            –2x – 4
            –2x – 4
            ───────
                 0
```

14) The correct answer is D.

If $5x – 2(x + 3) = 0$, then $x = ?$

To solve this type of problem, do the multiplication on the items in parentheses first.

$5x – 2(x + 3) = 0$

$5x – 2x – 6 = 0$

Then deal with the integers by putting them on one side of the equation as follows:

$5x – 2x – 6 + 6 = 0 + 6$

$3x = 6$

Then solve for x.

$3x = 6$

$x = 6 ÷ 3$

$x = 2$

15) The correct answer is D.

Simplify the following equation: $(x + 3y)^2$

This type of algebraic expression is known as a polynomial.

When multiplying polynomials, you should use the FOIL method.

This means that you multiply the terms two at a time from each of the two parts of the equation in this order:

First – Outside – Inside – Last

$(x + 3y)^2 = (x + 3y)(x + 3y)$

FIRST – Multiply the first term from the first set of parentheses with the first term from the second set of parentheses.

(x + 3y)(x + 3y)

$x \times x = x^2$

OUTSIDE – Multiply the first term from the first set of parentheses with the second term from the second set of parentheses.

(x + 3y)(x + **3y**)

$x \times 3y = 3xy$

INSIDE – Multiply the second term from the first set of parentheses with the first term from the second set of parentheses.

(x + **3y**)(**x** + 3y)

$3y \times x = 3xy$

LAST– Multiply the second term from the first set of parentheses with the second term from the second set of parentheses.

(x + **3y**)(x + **3y**)

$3y \times 3y = 9y^2$

Then we add all of the above products together to get the answer.

$x^2 + 3xy + 3xy + 9y^2 =$

$x^2 + 6xy + 9y^2$

16) The correct answer is A.

(x + 3y)(x – y) = ?

Remember to use the FOIL method when you multiply.

As you will see below, if a term or variable is subtracted within the parentheses, you have to keep the negative sign with it when you multiply.

FIRST: (**x** + 3y)(**x** – y)

$x \times x = x^2$

OUTSIDE: $(x + 3y)(x - y)$

$x \times -y = -xy$

INSIDE: $(x + 3y)(x - y)$

$3y \times x = 3xy$

LAST: $(x + 3y)(x - y)$

$3y \times -y = -3y^2$

Then add all of the above once you have completed FOIL.

$x^2 - xy + 3xy - 3y^2 =$

$x^2 + 2xy - 3y^2$

17) The correct answer is D.

What is the value of the expression $6x^2 - xy + y^2$ when $x = 5$ and $y = -1$?

To solve this problem, put in the values for x and y and multiply. Remember that two negatives together make a positive.

For example, $-(-5) = 5$

So, be careful when multiplying negative numbers.

$6x^2 - xy + y^2 =$

$(6 \times 5^2) - (5 \times -1) + (-1^2) =$

$(6 \times 5 \times 5) - (-5) + 1 =$

$(6 \times 25) + 5 + 1 =$

$150 + 5 + 1 = 156$

18) The correct answer is D.

Two people are going to work on a job. The first person will be paid $7.25 per hour. The second person will be paid $10.50 per hour. If A represents the number of hours the first person will work, and B represents the number of hours the second person will work, what equation represents the total cost of the wages for this job?

The two people are working at different costs per hour, so each person needs to be assigned a variable.

A is for the number of hours for the first person, and B is for the number of hours for the second person.

The cost for each person is calculated by taking the number of hours that the person works by the hourly wage for that person.

So, the equation for wages for the first person is (7.25 × A)

The equation for the wages for the second person is (10.50 × B)

The total cost of the wages for this job is the sum of the wages of these two people.

(7.25 × A) + (10.50 × B) =

(7.25A + 10.50B)

19) The correct answer is B.

$x^2 + xy - y = 41$ and $x = 5$. What is the value of y?

Questions like this are just a different type of "solving by elimination" question.

Substitute 5 for the value of x to solve.

$x^2 + xy - y = 41$

$5^2 + 5y - y = 41$

$25 + 5y - y = 41$

$25 - 25 + 5y - y = 41 - 25$

$5y - y = 16$

$4y = 16$

$4y ÷ 4 = 16 ÷ 4$

$y = 4$

20) The correct answer is D.

$20 - \dfrac{3x}{4} \geq 17$, then $x \leq ?$

In order to solve inequalities, deal with the whole numbers on each side of the equation first.

$20 - \dfrac{3x}{4} \geq 17$

$(20 - 20) - \dfrac{3x}{4} \geq 17 - 20$

$-\dfrac{3x}{4} \geq -3$

Then deal with the fraction.

$-\dfrac{3x}{4} \geq -3$

$\left(4 \times -\dfrac{3x}{4}\right) \geq -3 \times 4$

$-3x \geq -12$

Then deal with the remaining whole numbers.

$-3x \geq -12$

$-3x \div 3 \geq -12 \div 3$

$-x \geq -4$

Then deal with the negative number.

$-x \geq -4$

$-x + 4 \geq -4 + 4$

$-x + 4 \geq 0$

Finally, isolate the unknown variable as a positive number.

$-x + 4 \geq 0$

$-x + x + 4 \geq 0 + x$

$4 \geq x$

$x \leq 4$

21) The correct answer is A.

Factor: $18x^2 - 2x$

Remember that you see several factoring problems on the test.

You have to find the greatest common factor.

The factors of 18 are:

1 × 18 = 18

2 × 9 = 18

3 × 6 = 18

The factors of 2 are:

1 × **2** = 2

So, put the integer for the common factor on the outside of the parentheses.

$18x^2 - 2x = 2(\quad)$

Then put the correct values into the parentheses.

$18x^2 - 2x = 2(9x^2 - x)$

Now determine whether there are any common variables for the terms that remain in the parentheses.

So, for $(9x^2 - x)$ we can see that $9x^2$ and x have the variable x in common.

Now factor out x to solve.

$2(9x^2 - x) =$

$2x(9x - 1)$

22) The correct answer is D.

Simplify the following: $(5x^2 + 3x - 4) - (6x^2 - 5x + 8)$

Remember to perform the operations on the parentheses first and to be careful with negatives.

$(5x^2 + 3x - 4) - (6x^2 - 5x + 8) =$

$5x^2 + 3x - 4 - 6x^2 + 5x - 8$

Then place the terms containing x and y together.

$5x^2 - 6x^2 + 3x + 5x - 4 - 8$

Finally add or subtract the terms.

$5x^2 - 6x^2 + 3x + 5x - 4 - 8 =$

$-x^2 + 8x - 12$

23) The correct answer is A.

$(x - 4)(3x + 2) = ?$

This is another application of the FOIL method.

FIRST: $(\mathbf{x} - 4)(\mathbf{3x} + 2)$

$x \times 3x = 3x^2$

OUTSIDE: $(\mathbf{x} - 4)(3x + \mathbf{2})$

$x \times 2 = 2x$

INSIDE: $(x - \mathbf{4})(\mathbf{3x} + 2)$

$-4 \times 3x = -12x$

LAST: $(x - \mathbf{4})(3x + \mathbf{2})$

$-4 \times 2 = -8$

Then add all of the above once you have completed FOIL.

$3x^2 + 2x + -12x + -8 =$

$3x^2 + 2x - 12x - 8 =$

$3x^2 - 10x - 8$

24) The correct answer is B.

Simplify: $\sqrt{7} + 2\sqrt{7}$

In order to add square roots like this, you need to add the numbers in front of the square root sign.

If there is no number before the radical, then put in the number 1 because the radical will count only 1 time in that case.

$\sqrt{7} + 2\sqrt{7} =$

$1\sqrt{7} + 2\sqrt{7} =$

$3\sqrt{7}$

25) The correct answer is D.

Factor the following: $x^2 + x - 20$

This is a reverse FOIL type of problem.

For any problem like this, the answer will be in the following format: $(x + ?)(x - ?)$

We know that the terms in the parentheses have to be in that format because we can get a negative number, like –20 above, only if we multiply a negative number and a positive number.

Next, we will look at the factors of 20:

1 × 20 = 20

2 × 10 = 20

4 × 5 = 20

So, we know that we need to have a plus sign in one set of parentheses and a minus sign in the other set of parentheses because 20 is negative.

We also know that the factors of 20 need to be one number different than each other because the middle term is x, in other words $1x$.

The only factors of twenty that meet this criterion are 4 and 5.

Therefore the answer is $(x + 5)(x - 4)$.

26) The correct answer is C.

$(x - 4y)^2 = ?$

Here is another opportunity to practice the FOIL method.

$(x - 4y)^2 = (x - 4y)(x - 4y)$

FIRST: $(\mathbf{x} - 4y)(\mathbf{x} - 4y)$

$x \times x = x^2$

OUTSIDE: $(\mathbf{x} - 4y)(x - \mathbf{4y})$

$x \times -4y = -4xy$

INSIDE: $(x - \mathbf{4y})(\mathbf{x} - 4y)$

$-4y \times x = -4xy$

LAST: $(x - \mathbf{4y})(x - \mathbf{4y})$

$-4y \times -4y = 16y^2$

SOLUTION:

$x^2 - 8xy + 16y^2$

27) The correct answer is B.

If $4x - 3(x + 2) = -3$, then $x = ?$

Remember to do multiplication on the items in parentheses first.

$4x - 3(x + 2) = -3$

$4x - 3x - 6 = -3$

Then deal with the integers.

$4x - 3x - 6 + 6 = -3 + 6$

$4x - 3x = 3$

Then solve for x.

$4x - 3x = 3$

$x = 3$

28) The correct answer is A.

$(x^2 - x - 12) \div (x - 4) = ?$

In order to solve the problem, you have to do long division of the polynomial.

```
              x + 3
      ┌─────────────
x − 4 )x² − x − 12
       x² − 4x
       ─────────
            3x − 12
            3x − 12
            ───────
                  0
```

29) The correct answer is B.

Mark's final grade for a course is based on the grades from two tests, A and B. Test A counts toward 35% of his final grade. Test B counts toward 65% of his final grade. What equation is used to calculate Mark's final grade for this course?

The two tests are being given different percentages, so each test needs to have its own variable.

A for test A and B for test B.

Since A counts for 35% of the final grade, we set 35% to a decimal and put the decimal in front of the variable so that the variable will have the correct weight.

So, the value of test A is .35A

Test B counts for 65%, so the value of test B is .65B

The final grade is the sum of the values for the two tests.

So, we add the above products together to get our equation.

.35A + .65B

30) The correct answer is A.

What is the value of the expression $2x^2 + 3xy - y^2$ when $x = 3$ and $y = -3$?

Put in the values for x and y and multiply.

$2x^2 + 3xy - y^2 =$

$(2 \times 3^2) + (3 \times 3 \times -3) - (-3^2) =$

$(2 \times 3 \times 3) + (3 \times 3 \times -3) - (-3 \times -3) =$

$(2 \times 9) + (3 \times -9) - (9) =$

$18 + (-27) - 9 =$

$18 - 27 - 9 =$

$18 - 36 =$

-18

PERT Math Practice Test 2 – Answers:

1) The correct answer is C.

$\sqrt{2} \times \sqrt{3} = ?$

In order to multiply two square roots, multiply the numbers inside the square roots.

$2 \times 3 = 6$

Then put this result inside a square root symbol for your answer.

$\sqrt{6}$

2) The correct answer is C.

Simplify: $(x - 2y)(2x - y)$

Do not the word "simplify" confuse you. Just apply the FOIL method again.

FIRST: $(\mathbf{x} - 2y)(\mathbf{2x} - y)$

$x \times 2x = 2x^2$

OUTSIDE: $(\mathbf{x} - 2y)(2x - \mathbf{y})$

$x \times -y = -xy$

INSIDE: $(x - \mathbf{2y})(\mathbf{2x} - y)$

$-2y \times 2x = -4xy$

LAST: $(x - \mathbf{2y})(2x - \mathbf{y})$

$-2y \times -y = 2y^2$

SOLUTION:

$2x^2 + -xy + -4xy + 2y^2 =$

$2x^2 - xy - 4xy + 2y^2 =$

$2x^2 - 5xy + 2y^2$

3) The correct answer is D.

$20 + \frac{x}{4} \geq 22$, then $x \geq$?

Deal with the whole numbers first.

$20 + \frac{x}{4} \geq 22$

$20 - 20 + \frac{x}{4} \geq 22 - 20$

$\frac{x}{4} \geq 2$

Then eliminate the fraction.

$\frac{x}{4} \geq 2$

$4 \times \frac{x}{4} \geq 2 \times 4$

$x \geq 8$

4) The correct answer is A.

State the x and y intercepts that fall on the straight line represented by the following equation:

y = x + 6

Remember that the y intercept exists where the line crosses the y axis, so x = 0 for the y intercept.

Begin by substituting 0 for x.

y = x + 6

y = 0 + 6

y = 6

Therefore, the coordinates (0, 6) represent the y intercept.

On the other hand, the x intercept exists where the line crosses the x axis, so y = 0 for the x intercept.

Now substitute 0 for y.

y = x + 6

0 = x + 6

0 – 6 = x + 6 – 6

–6 = x

So, the coordinates (–6, 0) represent the x intercept.

5) The correct answer is D.

(5x + 7y) + (3x – 9y) = ?

First perform the operations on the parentheses.

(5x + 7y) + (3x – 9y) =

5x + 7y + 3x – 9y

Then place the x and y terms together.

5x + 7y + 3x – 9y =

5x + 3x + 7y – 9y

Finally add and subtract to simplify.

5x + 3x + 7y – 9y =

8x – 2y

6) The correct answer is C.

If 5x – 4(x + 2) = –2, then x = ?

Isolate the x variable in order to solve the problem.

5x – 4(x + 2) = –2

5x – 4x – 8 = –2

x – 8 = –2

$x - 8 + 8 = -2 + 8$

$x = 6$

7) The correct answer is D.

Simplify: $(x - y)(x + y)$

Remember to use FOIL when the instructions tell you to simplify.

FIRST: $(\mathbf{x} - y)(\mathbf{x} + y)$

$x \times x = x^2$

OUTSIDE: $(\mathbf{x} - y)(x + \mathbf{y})$

$x \times y = xy$

INSIDE: $(x - \mathbf{y})(\mathbf{x} + y)$

$-y \times x = -xy$

LAST: $(x - \mathbf{y})(x + \mathbf{y})$

$-y \times y = -y^2$

SOLUTION:

$x^2 + xy + - xy - y^2 =$

$x^2 - y^2$

8) The correct answer is D.

$\sqrt{8} \times \sqrt{2} = ?$

For radical problems like this one, remember that you have to multiply the numbers inside the square roots.

$8 \times 2 = 16$

Put this result inside a square root symbol, and then simplify, if possible.

$\sqrt{16} = 4$

9) The correct answer is C.

Factor the following: $2xy - 8x^2y + 6y^2x^2$

First, figure out what variables are common to each term of the equation.

Let's look at the equation again.

$2xy - 8x^2y + 6y^2x^2$

We can see that each term contains *x*. We can also see that each term contains *y*.

So, now let's factor out *xy*.

$2xy - 8x^2y + 6y^2x^2 =$

$xy(2 - 8x + 6xy)$

Then, think about integers. We can see that all of the terms inside the parentheses are divisible by 2.

Now let's factor out the 2. In order to do this, we divide each term inside the parentheses by 2.

$xy(2 - 8x + 6xy) =$

$2xy(1 - 4x + 3xy)$

10) The correct answer is C.

$(x + 3) - (4 - x) = ?$

This question is asking you to simplify the variables in the parentheses.

Do the operation on the second set of parentheses first.

$(x + 3) - (4 - x) =$

$x + 3 - 4 + x$

Now simplify for the common terms.

$x + 3 - 4 + x =$

$x + x + 3 - 4 =$

$2x - 1$

11) The correct answer is D.

If $x - 1 > 0$ and $y = x - 1$, then $y > ?$

Notice that both equations contain x – 1. Since the second equation has the equal sign, we can substitute y for x – 1 in the first equation.

x – 1 > 0

x – 1 = y

y > 0

12) The correct answer is A.

Find the coordinates (x, y) of the midpoint of the line segment on a graph that connects the points (–5, 3) and (3, –5).

Remember that in order to find midpoints on a line, you need to use the midpoint formula.

For two points on a graph (x_1, y_1) and (x_2, y_2), the midpoint is:

$(x_1 + x_2) \div 2$, $(y_1 + y_2) \div 2$

(–5 + 3) ÷ 2 = midpoint x, (3 + –5) ÷ 2 = midpoint y

–2 ÷ 2 = midpoint x, –2 ÷ 2 = midpoint y

–1 = midpoint x, –1 = midpoint y

13) The correct answer is C.

The price of socks is $2 per pair and the price of shoes is $25 per pair. Anna went shopping for socks and shoes, and she paid $85 in total. In this purchase, she bought 3 pairs of shoes. How many pairs of socks did she buy?

Remember to assign a different variable to each item.

Then make your equation by multiplying each variable by its price.

So, let's say that the number of pairs of socks is S and the number of pairs of shoes is H.

Your equation is:

(S × $2) + (H × $25) = $85

We know that the number of pairs of shoes is 3, so put that in the equation and solve it.

(S × $2) + (H × $25) = $85

($S \times \$2$) + ($3 \times \$25$) = $85

($S \times \$2$) + $75 = $85

($S \times \$2$) + 75 − 75 = $85 − $75

($S \times \$2$) = $10

$2S = \$10$

$2S \div 2 = \$10 \div 2$

$S = 5$

So, she bought 5 pairs of socks.

14) The correct answer is B.

Consider a two-dimensional linear graph where $x = 3$ and $y = 14$. The line crosses the y axis at 5. What is the slope of this line?

When you are provided with a set of coordinates and the y intercept, you need the slope-intercept formula in order to calculate the slope of a line.

$y = mx + b$

In the slope-intercept formula, m is the slope and b is the y intercept, which is the point where the line crosses the y axis.

Now solve for the numbers given in the problem.

$y = mx + b$

$14 = m3 + 5$

$14 − 5 = m3 + 5 − 5$

$9 = m3$

$9 \div 3 = m$

$3 = m$

15) The correct answer is C.

If $5 + 5(3\sqrt{x} + 4) = 55$, then $\sqrt{x}$ = ?

First, deal with the integers that are outside the parentheses.

$5 + 5(3\sqrt{x} + 4) = 55$

$5 + 15\sqrt{x} + 20 = 55$

$25 + 15\sqrt{x} = 55$

$25 - 25 + 15\sqrt{x} = 55 - 25$

$15\sqrt{x} = 30$

Then divide in order to isolate $\sqrt{x}$.

$15\sqrt{x} = 30$

$(15\sqrt{x}) \div 15 = 30 \div 15$

$\sqrt{x} = 2$

16) The correct answer is D.

Factor the following equation: $6xy - 12x^2y - 24y^2x^2$

Remember to ask yourself: What variables are common to each term of the equation?

We can see that each term contains *x*. We can also see that each term contains *y*.

So, now let's factor out *xy*.

$6xy - 12x^2y - 24y^2x^2 =$

$xy(6 - 12x - 24xy)$

Then, think about integers. We can see that all of the terms inside the parentheses are divisible by 6.

So, factor out the 6 by dividing each term inside the parentheses by 6.

$xy(6 - 12x - 24xy) =$

$6xy(1 - 2x - 4xy)$

17) The correct answer is D.

If x − 5 < 0 and y < x + 10, then y < ?

First solve the equation for x.

x − 5 < 0

x − 5 + 5 < 0 + 5

x < 5

Then solve for y by replacing x with its value.

y < x + 10

y < 5 + 10

y < 15

18) The correct answer is A.

Find the x and y intercepts of the following equation: $4x^2 + 9y^2 = 36$

Remember that for questions about x and y intercepts, you need to substitute 0 for x and then substitute 0 for y in order to solve the problem.

Here is the solution for y intercept:

$4x^2 + 9y^2 = 36$

$4(0x^2) + 9y^2 = 36$

$0 + 9y^2 = 36$

$9y^2 \div 9 = 36 \div 9$

$y^2 = 4$

$y = 2$

So, the y intercept is (0, 2)

Here is the solution for x intercept:

$4x^2 + 9y^2 = 36$

$4x^2 + 9(0y^2) = 36$

$4x^2 + 0 = 36$

$4x^2 \div 4 = 36 \div 4$

$x^2 = 9$

$x = 3$

So the x intercept is (3, 0)

19) The correct answer is D.

Find the midpoint between the following coordinates: (2, 2) and (4, −6)

Use the midpoint formula.

For two points on a graph (x_1, y_1) and (x_2, y_2), the midpoint is:

$(x_1 + x_2) \div 2$, $(y_1 + y_2) \div 2$

$(2 + 4) \div 2$ = midpoint x, $(2 − 6) \div 2$ = midpoint y

$6 \div 2$ = midpoint x, $−4 \div 2$ = midpoint y

3 = midpoint x, −2 = midpoint y

20) The correct answer is D.

If $4 + 3(2\sqrt{x} - 3) = 25$, then x = ?

Deal with the integers that are outside the parentheses first.

$4 + 3(2\sqrt{x} - 3) = 25$

$4 - 4 + 3(2\sqrt{x} - 3) = 25 - 4$

$3(2\sqrt{x} - 3) = 21$

Then carry out the operations for the parenthetical terms.

$3(2\sqrt{x} - 3) = 21$

$6\sqrt{x} - 9 = 21$

$6\sqrt{x} - 9 + 9 = 21 + 9$

$6\sqrt{x} = 30$

Then isolate $\sqrt{x}$.

$6\sqrt{x} \div 6 = 30 \div 6$

$\sqrt{x} = 5$

However, we are solving for x, not for $\sqrt{x}$.

So, we have to square each side of the equation in order to solve the problem.

$\sqrt{x} \times \sqrt{x} = 5 \times 5$

$x = 25$

21) The correct answer is B.

The Smith family is having lunch in a diner. They buy hot dogs and hamburgers to eat. The hot dogs cost $2.50 each, and the hamburgers cost $4 each. They buy 3 hamburgers. They also buy hot dogs. The total value of their purchase is $22. How many hot dogs did they buy?

Remember to assign variables to the items and then multiply each variable by its price.

The number of hot dogs is *D* and the number of hamburgers is *H*.

So, your equation is: (*D* × $2.50) + (*H* × $4) = $22

The number of hamburgers is 3, so put that in the equation and solve it.

(*D* × $2.50) + (*H* × $4) = $22

(*D* × $2.50) + (3 × $4) = $22

(*D* × $2.50) + 12 = $22

(*D* × $2.50) + 12 − 12 = $22 − 12

(*D* × $2.50) = $10

$2.50*D* = $10

$2.50*D* ÷ $2.50 = $10 ÷ $2.50

D = 4

22) The correct answer is D.

Simplify: $(x + 5) - (x^2 - 2x)$

First, remove the parentheses, paying attention to the negative sign in front of the second set of parentheses.

$(x + 5) - (x^2 - 2x) =$

$x + 5 - x^2 + 2x$

Now simplify for the common terms.

$x + 5 - x^2 + 2x =$

$x + 2x + 5 - x^2 =$

$x + 2x - x^2 + 5 =$

$3x - x^2 + 5$

23) The correct answer is D.

$(-3x^2 + 7x + 2) - (x^2 - 5) = ?$

Remove the negative sign in front of the second set of parentheses by performing the operations on the double negative.

$(-3x^2 + 7x + 2) - (x^2 - 5) =$

$(-3x^2 + 7x + 2) - x^2 + 5$

Then remove the first set of parentheses.

$(-3x^2 + 7x + 2) - x^2 + 5 =$

$-3x^2 + 7x + 2 - x^2 + 5$

Then group like terms together to solve the problem.

$-3x^2 + 7x + 2 - x^2 + 5 =$

$-3x^2 - x^2 + 7x + 2 + 5 =$

$-4x^2 + 7x + 7$

24) The correct answer is B.

$$\frac{x^2+10x+16}{x^2+11x+18} \times \frac{x^2+9x}{x^2+17x+72} = ?$$

For this type of problem, first you need to find the factors of the numerators and denominators of each fraction.

As we have explained in the review section at the beginning of this book, when there are only addition signs in the rational expression, the factors will be in the following format:

(+)(+)

STEP 1: The numerator of the first fraction is $x^2+10x+16$, so the final integer is 16.

The factors of 16 are:

1 × 16 = 16

2 × 8 = 16

4 × 4 = 16

Then add these factors together to discover what integer you need to use in front of the second term of the expression.

1 + 16 = 17

2 + 8 = 10

4 + 4 = 8

2 and 8 satisfy both parts of the equation.

Therefore, the factors of $x^2+10x+16$ are $(x+2)(x+8)$.

Now factor the other parts of the problem.

STEP 2: The denominator of the first fraction is $x^2+11x+18$, so the final integer is 18.

The factors of 18 are:

1 × 18 = 18

2 × 9 = 18

3 × 6 = 18

Add these factors together to find the integer to use in front of the second term of the expression.

1 + 18 = 19

2 + 9 = 11

3 + 6 = 9

Therefore, the factors of $x^2 + 11x + 18$ are $(x+2)(x+9)$.

STEP 3: The numerator of the second fraction is $x^2 + 9x$, so there is no final integer.

Because x is common to both terms of the expression, the factor will be in this format:

$x(x + \quad)$

Therefore, the factors of $x^2 + 9x$ are $x(x+9)$.

STEP 4: The denominator of the second fraction is $x^2 + 17x + 72$, so the final integer is 72.

The factors of 72 are:

1 × 72 = 72

2 × 36 = 72

3 × 24 = 72

4 × 18 = 72

6 × 12 = 72

8 × 9 = 72

Add these factors together to find the integer to use in front of the second term of the expression.

1 + 72 = 73

2 + 36 = 38

3 + 24 = 27

4 + 18 = 22

6 + 12 = 18

8 + 9 = 17

Therefore, the factors of $x^2 + 17x + 72$ are $(x+8)(x+9)$.

Now we can solve our problem with the factors that we have found in each step.

$$\frac{x^2 + 10x + 16}{x^2 + 11x + 18} = \frac{(x+2)(x+8)}{(x+2)(x+9)} \qquad \frac{x^2 + 9x}{x^2 + 17x + 72} = \frac{x(x+9)}{(x+8)(x+9)}$$

So, replace the polynomials in the question with their factors from above.

$$\frac{x^2 + 10x + 16}{x^2 + 11x + 18} \times \frac{x^2 + 9x}{x^2 + 17x + 72} =$$

$$\frac{(x+2)(x+8)}{(x+2)(x+9)} \times \frac{x(x+9)}{(x+8)(x+9)}$$

Then for each fraction, you need to simplify by removing the common factors.

Remove $(x + 2)$ from the first fraction.

$$\frac{(x+2)(x+8)}{(x+2)(x+9)} \times \frac{x(x+9)}{(x+8)(x+9)} =$$

$$\frac{(x+8)}{(x+9)} \times \frac{x(x+9)}{(x+8)(x+9)}$$

Then remove $(x + 9)$ from the second fraction.

$$\frac{(x+8)}{(x+9)} \times \frac{x(x+9)}{(x+8)(x+9)} =$$

$$\frac{(x+8)}{(x+9)} \times \frac{x}{(x+8)}$$

Once you have simplified each fraction as above, perform the operation indicated. In this problem, you need to multiply the two fractions.

$$\frac{(x+8)}{(x+9)} \times \frac{x}{(x+8)} = \frac{x(x+8)}{(x+9)(x+8)}$$

When you have completed the operation, you need to check to see whether any further simplification is possible.

In this case, the fraction may be further simplified because the numerator and denominator share the common factor $(x + 8)$.

$$\frac{x(x+8)}{(x+9)(x+8)} = \frac{x}{x+9}$$

So, our final answer is $\frac{x}{x+9}$

25) The correct answer is C.

$\sqrt{5b-4} = 4$ What is the value of b?

In order to find the value of a variable inside a square root sign, your first step is to square each side of the equation.

$$\sqrt{(5b-4)^2} = 4^2$$

$$5b - 4 = 16$$

Then place the integers on one side of the equation.

$$5b - 4 = 16$$

$$5b - 4 + 4 = 16 + 4$$

$$5b = 20$$

Then isolate the variable to one side of the equation in order to solve the problem.

$$5b \div 5 = 20 \div 5$$

$$b = 4$$

26) The correct answer is D.

$$\frac{5z-5}{z} \div \frac{6z-6}{5z^2} = ?$$

When dividing fractions, you need to invert the second fraction and then multiply the two fractions together.

$$\frac{5z-5}{z} \div \frac{6z-6}{5z^2} =$$

$$\frac{5z-5}{z} \times \frac{5z^2}{6z-6}$$

When multiplying fractions, you multiply the numerator of the first fraction by the numerator of the second fraction and denominator of the first fraction by the denominator of the second fraction.

$$\frac{5z-5}{z} \times \frac{5z^2}{6z-6} =$$

$$\frac{5z^2(5z-5)}{z(6z-6)} =$$

$$\frac{25z^3 - 25z^2}{6z^2 - 6z}$$

Then look at the numerator and denominator from the result of the previous step to see if you can factor and simplify.

In this case, the numerator and denominator have the common factor of $(z^2 - z)$.

$$\frac{25z^3 - 25z^2}{6z^2 - 6z} =$$

$$\frac{25z(z^2 - z)}{6(z^2 - z)} =$$

$$\frac{25z}{6}$$

27) The correct answer is C.

If $c = \dfrac{a}{1-b}$, then b = ?

First you need to get rid of the fraction. To eliminate the fraction, multiply each side of the equation by the denominator of the fraction.

$$c = \frac{a}{1-b}$$

$$c \times (1-b) = \frac{a}{1-b} \times (1-b)$$

$$c \times (1-b) = a$$

Then simplify the side of the equation with the variable that you need to isolate, in this case b.

$$c \times (1-b) = a$$

$$c(1-b) \div c = a \div c$$

$$1 - b = \frac{a}{c}$$

Then isolate b by dealing with the integer and the negative sign in order to solve the problem.

$$1 - b = \frac{a}{c}$$

$$1 - 1 - b = \frac{a}{c} - 1$$

$$-b = \frac{a}{c} - 1$$

$$-b \times -1 = \left(\frac{a}{c} - 1\right) \times -1$$

$$b = -\frac{a}{c} + 1$$

28) The correct answer is C.

$$\sqrt{14x^5} \times \sqrt{6x^3} = ?$$

First do the multiplication of the integers. Remember that when there are exponents inside the square root signs, you add the exponents together.

So, multiply the integers and add the exponents.

$$\sqrt{14x^5} \times \sqrt{6x^3} = \sqrt{84x^8}$$

Then factor the integer inside the square root sign and simplify.

Remember that if you are finding factors for integers inside a radical, you should look for factors that have whole number square roots.

4 is the only factor of 84 that has a whole number as a square root because the square root of 4 is 2.

So, we factor as follows:

$$\sqrt{84x^8} = \sqrt{4 \times 21x^8}$$

Then we simplify like this:

$$\sqrt{4 \times 21x^8} =$$

$$\sqrt{(2 \times 2) \times 21x^8} =$$

$$2\sqrt{21x^8}$$

In order to simplify further, we need to deal with the x term.

Remember that the square root of any number is that number to the ½ power.

For example, $\sqrt{x} = x^{\frac{1}{2}}$

So, we can further simplify the x term in our problem.

$$2\sqrt{21x^8} =$$

$$2 \times \sqrt{21} \times x^{\frac{8}{2}}$$

$2 \times \sqrt{21} \times x^4$

$2x^4 \sqrt{21}$

28) The correct answer is C.

$\sqrt{14x^5} \times \sqrt{6x^3} = ?$

First do the multiplication of the integers. Remember that when there are exponents inside the square root signs, you add the exponents together.

So, multiply the integers and add the exponents.

$\sqrt{14x^5} \times \sqrt{6x^3} = \sqrt{84x^8}$

Then factor the integer inside the square root sign and simplify.

Remember that if you are finding factors for integers inside a radical, you should look for factors that have whole number square roots.

4 is the only factor of 84 that has a whole number as a square root because the square root of 4 is 2.

So, we factor as follows:

$\sqrt{84x^8} = \sqrt{4 \times 21 x^8}$

Then we simplify like this:

$\sqrt{4 \times 21 x^8} =$

$\sqrt{(2 \times 2) \times 21 x^8} =$

$2\sqrt{21 x^8}$

In order to simplify further, we need to deal with the x term.

Remember that the square root of any number is that number to the ½ power.

For example, $\sqrt{x} = x^{\frac{1}{2}}$

So, we can further simplify the x term in our problem.

$2\sqrt{21x^8} =$

$2 \times \sqrt{21} \times x^{\frac{8}{2}}$

$2 \times \sqrt{21} \times x^4$

$2x^4 \sqrt{21}$

29) The correct answer is D.

$8ab^2(3ab^4 + 2b) = ?$

Remember to multiply the integers, but to add the exponents.

Also remember that any variable times itself is equal to that variable squared. For example, a × a = a²

$8ab^2(3ab^4 + 2b) =$

$(8ab^2 \times 3ab^4) + (8ab^2 \times 2b) =$

$24a^2b^6 + 16ab^3$

30) The correct answer is D.

Perform the operation and express as one fraction: $\dfrac{5}{12x} + \dfrac{4}{10x^2} = ?$

First you have to find the lowest common denominator (LCD).

For denominators that have integers and variables, you need two steps in order to find the LCD.

(1) Deal with the integers in the denominator.

(2) Then deal with the variable.

In order to find the LCD, ask yourself: What is the smallest possible number that is divisible by both 12 and by 10? The answer is 60.

Alternatively, find the factors of 12 and 10, and then multiply by the factor that they do not have in common.

12 = 2 × 6 and 10 = 2 × 5, so multiply 12 by 5 and 10 by 6 to arrive at 60 for the integer part of the denominator.

Then deal with the variable. $x = x \times 1$ and $x^2 = x \times x$, so multiply $x^2 \times 1$ and $x \times x$, to get x^2 for the variable part of the denominator.

Then put together the product of the LCD for the integer and the product of the LCD for the variable.

60 for the integer

x^2 for the variable

So, the LCD is $60x^2$.

$$\frac{5}{12x} + \frac{4}{10x^2} =$$

$$\left(\frac{5}{12x} \times \frac{5x}{5x}\right) + \left(\frac{4}{10x^2} \times \frac{6}{6}\right) = =$$

$$\frac{25x}{60x^2} + \frac{24}{60x^2} =$$

$$\frac{25x + 24}{60x^2}$$

PERT Math Practice Test 3 – Answers:

1) The correct answer is A.

In the standard (x, y) plane, what is the distance between $(3\sqrt{3}, -1)$ and $(6\sqrt{3}, 2)$?

To solve problems asking for the distance between two points (x_1, y_1) and (x_2, y_2), you need to use the distance formula.

$$d = \sqrt{(x_2 - x_1)^2 + (y_2 - y_1)^2}$$

Now we need to put in the values stated: $(3\sqrt{3}, -1)$ and $(6\sqrt{3}, 2)$

$$d = \sqrt{(6\sqrt{3} - 3\sqrt{3})^2 + (2 - -1)^2}$$

$$d = \sqrt{(3\sqrt{3})^2 + (3)^2}$$

$$d = \sqrt{(9 \times 3) + 9}$$

$$d = \sqrt{27 + 9}$$

$$d = \sqrt{36}$$

$$d = 6$$

2) The correct answer is D.

Perform the operation: $\sqrt{5}(\sqrt{20} - \sqrt{5})$

Multiply the radical in front of the parentheses by each radical inside the parentheses.

$\sqrt{5}(\sqrt{20} - \sqrt{5}) =$

$(\sqrt{5} \times \sqrt{20}) - (\sqrt{5} \times \sqrt{5}) =$

$\sqrt{100} - \sqrt{25}$

Then find the square roots and subtract.

$\sqrt{100} - \sqrt{25} =$

$\sqrt{10 \times 10} - \sqrt{5 \times 5} =$

$10 - 5 = 5$

3) The correct answer is B.

$8^7 \times 8^3 = ?$

This question tests your knowledge of exponent laws.

First look to see whether your base number is the same on each part of the equation.

In this question, 8 is the base number for each part of the equation.

If the base number is the same, and the problem asks you to multiply, you simply add the exponents.

$8^7 \times 8^3 =$

$8^{(7 + 3)} =$

8^{10}

If the base number is the same, and the problem asks you to divide, you subtract the exponents.

4) The correct answer is A.

Solve by elimination:

$x + 5y = 24$

$8x + 2y = 40$

In order to solve by elimination, you need to subtract the second equation from the first equation.

Look at the term containing x in the second equation. We have $8x$ in the second equation.

In order to eliminate the term containing x, we need to multiply the first equation by 8.

$x + 5y = 24$

$(8 \times x) + (5y \times 8) = (24 \times 8)$

$8x + 40y = 192$

Now do the subtraction.

$$\begin{aligned} 8x + 40y &= 192 \\ -(8x + 2y &= 40) \\ \hline 38y &= 152 \end{aligned}$$

Then solve for y.

$38y = 152$

$38y \div 38 = 152 \div 38$

$y = 4$

Now put the value for *y* into the first equation and solve for *x*.

$x + 5y = 24$

$x + (5 \times 4) = 24$

$x + 20 = 24$

$x + 20 - 20 = 24 - 20$

$x = 4$

Therefore, $x = 4$ and $y = 4$, so the answer is (4, 4).

5) The correct answer is C.

Perform the operation: $(4x - 3)(5x^2 + 12x + 11) = ?$

For problems like this one, you need to multiply the first term in the first set of parentheses by all of the terms in the second set of parentheses.

Then multiply the second term in the first set of parentheses by all of the terms in the second set of parentheses.

So, you need to multiply as shown.

$(4x - 3)(5x^2 + 12x + 11) =$

$[(4x \times 5x^2) + (4x \times 12x) + (4x \times 11)] - [(3 \times 5x^2) + (3 \times 12x) + (3 \times 11)] =$

$(20x^3 + 48x^2 + 44x) - (15x^2 + 36x + 33)$

Then simplify, remembering to be careful about the negative sign in front of the second set of parentheses.

$(20x^3 + 48x^2 + 44x) - (15x^2 + 36x + 33) =$

$(20x^3 + 48x^2 + 44x) - 15x^2 - 36x - 33 =$

$20x^3 + 48x^2 - 15x^2 + 44x - 36x - 33 =$

$20x^3 + 33x^2 + 8x - 33$

6) The correct answer is C.

Remember to multiply the integers inside the two square root signs and add the exponents when multiplying the two terms.

$\sqrt{6x^3} \sqrt{24x^5} =$

$\sqrt{144x^8}$

Then find the square root, if possible.

$\sqrt{144x^8} =$

$\sqrt{(12 \times 12)(x^4 \times x^4)} =$

$12x^4$

7) The correct answer is B.

$\sqrt{18} + 3\sqrt{32} + 5\sqrt{8} = ?$

Factor the integers inside each of the square root signs.

Remember that you need to find a squared number for one of the factors for each radical.

$\sqrt{18} + 3\sqrt{32} + 5\sqrt{8} =$

$$\sqrt{2 \times 9} + 3\sqrt{2 \times 16} + 5\sqrt{2 \times 4} =$$

$$\sqrt{2 \times (3 \times 3)} + 3\sqrt{2 \times (4 \times 4)} + 5\sqrt{2 \times (2 \times 2)} =$$

$$3\sqrt{2} + (3 \times 4)\sqrt{2} + (5 \times 2)\sqrt{2}$$

Then do the multiplication and addition.

$$3\sqrt{2} + (3 \times 4)\sqrt{2} + (5 \times 2)\sqrt{2} =$$

$$3\sqrt{2} + 12\sqrt{2} + 10\sqrt{2} =$$

$$(3 + 12 + 10)\sqrt{2} =$$

$$25\sqrt{2}$$

8) The correct answer is D.

What equation represents the slope-intercept formula for the following data?

Through (4, 5); $m = -3/5$

You will remember that the slope intercept formula is: $y = mx + b$

Remember that *m* is the slope and *b* is the *y* intercept.

You will also need the slope formula: $m = \dfrac{y_2 - y_1}{x_2 - x_1}$

We are given the slope, as well as the point (4,5), so first we need to put those points into the slope formula.

We are doing this in order to solve for *b*, which is not provided in the facts of the problem.

$$\dfrac{y_2 - y_1}{x_2 - x_1} = -\dfrac{3}{5}$$

$$\dfrac{5 - y_1}{4 - x_1} = -\dfrac{3}{5}$$

Then eliminate the denominator.

$$(4-x_1)\frac{5-y_1}{4-x_1} = -\frac{3}{5}(4-x_1)$$

$$5-y_1 = -\frac{3}{5}(4-x_1)$$

Now put in 0 for x_1 in the slope formula in order to find b, which is the y intercept (the point at which the line crosses the y axis).

$$5-y_1 = -\frac{3}{5}(4-x_1)$$

$$5-y_1 = -\frac{3}{5}(4-0)$$

$$5-y_1 = -\frac{3 \times 4}{5}$$

$$5-y_1 = -\frac{12}{5}$$

$$5-5-y_1 = -\frac{12}{5}-5$$

$$-y_1 = -\frac{12}{5}-5$$

$$-y_1 \times -1 = \left(-\frac{12}{5}-5\right) \times -1$$

$$y_1 = \frac{12}{5}+5$$

$$y_1 = \frac{12}{5}+\left(5 \times \frac{5}{5}\right)$$

$$y_1 = \frac{12}{5}+\frac{25}{5}$$

$$y_1 = \frac{12+25}{5}$$

$$y_1 = \frac{37}{5}$$

Remember that the *y* intercept (known in the slope-intercept formula as the variable *b*) exists when *x* is equal to 0.

We have put in the value of 0 for *x* in the equation above, so $b = \frac{37}{5}$

Now put the value for *b* into the slope intercept formula.

y = mx + b

$$y = -\frac{3}{5}x + \frac{37}{5}$$

9) The correct answer is D.

For all $a \neq b$, $\dfrac{\dfrac{5a}{b}}{\dfrac{2a}{a-b}} = ?$

When you have fractions in the numerator and denominator of another fraction, you can divide the two fractions as follows:

$$\dfrac{\dfrac{5a}{b}}{\dfrac{2a}{a-b}} = \frac{5a}{b} \div \frac{2a}{a-b}$$

Then invert and multiply just like you would for any other fraction.

$$\frac{5a}{b} \div \frac{2a}{a-b} =$$

$$\frac{5a}{b} \times \frac{a-b}{2a} =$$

132

$$\frac{5a^2 - 5ab}{2ab}$$

Then simplify, if possible.

$$\frac{5a^2 - 5ab}{2ab} =$$

$$\frac{a(5a - 5b)}{a(2b)} =$$

$$\frac{5a - 5b}{2b}$$

10) The correct answer is D.

Perform the operation and express as one fraction: $\frac{1}{a+1} + \frac{1}{a}$

Find the lowest common denominator.

$$\frac{1}{a+1} + \frac{1}{a} =$$

$$\left(\frac{1}{a+1} \times \frac{a}{a}\right) + \left(\frac{1}{a} \times \frac{a+1}{a+1}\right) =$$

$$\frac{a}{a^2 + a} + \frac{a+1}{a^2 + a}$$

Then simplify, if possible

$$\frac{a}{a^2 + a} + \frac{a+1}{a^2 + a} =$$

$$\frac{a + a + 1}{a^2 + a} =$$

$$\frac{2a + 1}{a^2 + a}$$

11) The correct answer is B.

$$\frac{\sqrt{48}}{3} + \frac{5\sqrt{5}}{6} = ?$$

Find the lowest common denominator.

$$\frac{\sqrt{48}}{3} + \frac{5\sqrt{5}}{6} =$$

$$\left(\frac{\sqrt{48}}{3} \times \frac{2}{2}\right) + \frac{5\sqrt{5}}{6} =$$

$$\frac{2\sqrt{48}}{6} + \frac{5\sqrt{5}}{6}$$

Then simplify, if possible.

$$\frac{2\sqrt{48}}{6} + \frac{5\sqrt{5}}{6} =$$

$$\frac{2\sqrt{16 \times 3} + 5\sqrt{5}}{6} =$$

$$\frac{2\sqrt{(4 \times 4) \times 3} + 5\sqrt{5}}{6} =$$

$$\frac{(2 \times 4)\sqrt{3} + 5\sqrt{5}}{6} =$$

$$\frac{8\sqrt{3} + 5\sqrt{5}}{6}$$

12) The correct answer is D.

For all $x \neq 0$ and $y \neq 0$, $\dfrac{4x}{\dfrac{1}{xy}} = ?$

When the denominator of a fraction contains another fraction, treat the main fraction as the division sign.

$$\frac{4x}{1/xy} = 4x \div 1/xy$$

Then invert and multiply as usual.

$$4x \div 1/xy = 4x \times xy/1$$

$$4x \times xy/1 = 4x \times xy$$

$$4x \times xy = 4x^2 y$$

13) The correct answer is C.

$10a^2b^3c \div 2ab^2c^2 = ?$

First perform the division on the integers.

$10 \div 2 = 5$

Then do the division on the other variables.

$a^2 \div a = a$

$b^3 \div b^2 = b$

$c \div c^2 = \dfrac{1}{c}$

Then multiply these together to get the solution.

$$5 \times a \times b \times \frac{1}{c} =$$

$$\frac{5ab}{c} = 5ab \div c$$

14) The correct answer is D.

If x and y are positive integers, the expression $\dfrac{1}{\sqrt{x} - \sqrt{y}}$ is equivalent to what expression?

First of all, you have to eliminate the radicals in the denominator by factoring.

When you have two different variables in a rational expression such as x and y in this problem and your second variable is negative, your factored equation will be in the format (+)(−).

We know that one sign will be positive and the other will be negative when we factor because we can get a negative product only when we multiply a positive number with a negative number. So, we will multiply the denominator as follows:

$$\left(\sqrt{x}+\sqrt{y}\right)\left(\sqrt{x}-\sqrt{y}\right)$$

We can swap the order of the sets of parentheses to make the multiplication a bit easier to follow.

$$\left(\sqrt{x}+\sqrt{y}\right)\left(\sqrt{x}-\sqrt{y}\right)=$$

$$\left(\sqrt{x}-\sqrt{y}\right)\left(\sqrt{x}+\sqrt{y}\right)$$

Now we are ready to solve the problem.

$$\frac{1}{\sqrt{x}-\sqrt{y}}=$$

$$\frac{1}{\sqrt{x}-\sqrt{y}} \times \frac{\sqrt{x}+\sqrt{y}}{\sqrt{x}+\sqrt{y}}$$

Simplify the numerator and multiply the radicals in the denominator by using the FOIL method.

$$\frac{1}{\sqrt{x}-\sqrt{y}} \times \frac{\sqrt{x}+\sqrt{y}}{\sqrt{x}+\sqrt{y}}=$$

$$\frac{\sqrt{x}+\sqrt{y}}{\sqrt{x}^2+\sqrt{xy}-\sqrt{xy}-\sqrt{y}^2}=$$

$$\frac{\sqrt{x}+\sqrt{y}}{(\sqrt{x})^2-(\sqrt{y})^2}$$

Then simplify the denominator.

$$\frac{\sqrt{x}+\sqrt{y}}{(\sqrt{x})^2-(\sqrt{y})^2}=$$

$$\frac{\sqrt{x}+\sqrt{y}}{x-y}$$

15) The correct answer is D.

$(2+\sqrt{6})^2 = ?$

Don't worry about the radical. This is just another type of FOIL problem.

$(2+\sqrt{6})^2 =$

$(2+\sqrt{6})(2+\sqrt{6}) =$

First . . . Outside . . Inside . . . Last

$(2\times 2)+(2\times\sqrt{6})+(2\times\sqrt{6})+(\sqrt{6}\times\sqrt{6}) =$

$(2\times 2)+(2\sqrt{6}+2\sqrt{6})+\sqrt{6}^2 =$

$4+4\sqrt{6}+6 =$

$10+4\sqrt{6}$

16) The correct answer is D.

$\sqrt[3]{5} \times \sqrt[3]{7} = ?$

Remember for problems like this, you need to multiply the amounts inside the square root sign, but leave the cube root as it is.

$\sqrt[3]{5} \times \sqrt[3]{7} = \sqrt[3]{35}$

17) The correct answer is B.

What is the value of $\dfrac{x-3}{2-x}$ when $x = 1$?

Substitute 1 for x.

$$\frac{x-3}{2-x} =$$

$$\frac{1-3}{2-1} =$$

$(1-3) \div (2-1) =$

$-2 \div 1 =$

-2

18) The correct answer is C.

The term PPM, pulses per minute, is used to determine how many heartbeats an individual has every 60 seconds. In order to calculate PPM, the pulse is taken for ten seconds, represented by variable P. What equation is used to calculate PPM?

Since there are 60 seconds in a minute, and pulse is measured in 10 second units, we divide the seconds as follows: $60 \div 10 = 6$

Accordingly, the PPM is calculated by talking P times 6: PPM = P6

19) The correct answer is D.

Medical authorities have recommended that an individual's ideal PPM is 60. What equation is used to calculate by how much a person's PPM exceeds the ideal PPM?

The PPM is calculated as in the previous problem.

In order to find the excess amount, we deduct the ideal PPM of 60 from the patient's actual PPM.

PPM – 60

20) The correct answer is A.

A runner of a 100 mile endurance race ran at a speed of 5 miles per hour for the first 80 miles of the race and *x* miles per hour for the last 20 miles of the race. What equation represents the runner's average speed for the entire race?

Miles per hour (MPH) is calculated as follows:

miles ÷ hours = MPH

So, if we have the MPH and the miles traveled, we need to change the above equation in order to calculate the hours.

miles ÷ hours = MPH

miles ÷ hours × hours = MPH × hours

miles = MPH × hours

miles ÷ MPH = (MPH × hours) ÷ MPH

miles ÷ MPH = hours

In other words, we divide the number of miles by the miles per hour to get the time for each part of the race.

So, for the first part of the race, the hours are calculated as follows:

80 ÷ 5

For the second part of the race, we take the remaining mileage and divide by the unknown variable.

20 ÷ x

Since the race is divided into two parts, these two results added together equal the total time.

Total time = [(80 ÷ 5) + (20 ÷ x)]

The total amount of miles for the race is then divided by the total time to get the average miles per hour for the entire race.

That is because MPH is calculated as follows:

MPH = miles ÷ hours

We have a 100 mile race, so the result is:

100 ÷ [(80 ÷ 5) + (20 ÷ x)]

21) The correct answer is D.

$3^4 \times 3^3 = ?$

Remember to add the exponents when multiplying.

$3^4 \times 3^3 = 3^{3+4} = 3^7$

22) The correct answer is D.

The number of bottles of soda that a soft drink factory can produce during *D* number of days using production method A is represented by the following equation:

$D^5 + 12,000$

Alternatively, the number of bottles of soda that can be produced using production method B is represented by this equation:

$D \times 10,000$

What is the largest number of bottles of soda that can be produced by the factory during a 10 day period?

First we have to calculate the output for our first production method.

For 10 days:

$D^5 + 12,000 =$

$10^5 + 12,000 =$

$100,000 + 12,000 =$

$112,000$

Then we have to calculate the output for the other production method.

$10 \times 10,000 = 100,000$

112,000 is greater than the 100,000 amount that method B yields.

So, the greatest amount of production for 10 days is 112,000 bottles.

23) The correct answer is C.

$5^8 \div 5^2 = ?$

If the base number is the same, and the problem asks you to divide, you subtract the exponents.

$5^8 \div 5^2 = 5^{8-2} = 5^6$

24) The correct answer is C.

The facts of our problem are as follows:

A driver travels at 60 miles per hour for two and a half hours before her car fails to start at a service station.

The driver has to wait two hours while the car is repaired before she can continue driving.

She then drives at 75 miles an hour for the remainder of her journey.

She is traveling to Denver, and her journey is 240 miles in total.

If she left home at 6:00 am, what time will she arrive in Denver?

So, calculate the time for each part of the problem.

Time spent before needing the repair: 2.5 hours

Time spent waiting for the repair: 2 hours

Then we have to calculate the remaining time spent traveling to Denver.

We know that she traveled 150 miles before the repair.

Miles traveled before needing the repair: 60 MPH × 2.5 hours = 150 miles traveled

If the journey is 240 miles in total, she has 90 miles remaining after the car is repaired.

240 − 150 = 90

If she then travels at 75 miles an hour for 90 miles, the time she spends is:

90 ÷ 75 = 1.2 hours

Be careful with the decimal point!

There are 60 minutes in an hour, so 1.2 hours is 1 hour and 12 minutes because 60 minutes × 0.20 = 12 minutes.

The time spent traveling after the repair is 1 hour and 12 minutes.

Now add together all of the times to get your answer.

Time spent before needing the repair: 2.5 hours = 2 hours and 30 minutes

Time spent waiting for the repair: 2 hours

The time spent traveling after the repair: 1 hour and 12 minutes.

Total time: 5 hours and 42 minutes

If she left home at 6:00 am, she will arrive in Denver at 11:42 am.

25) The correct answer is B.

Which one of the following is a solution to the following ordered pairs of equations?

$y = -2x - 1$

$y = x - 4$

A) (0, 1)

B) (1, −3)

C) (4, 0)

D) (1, 3)

Plug in values for x and y to see if they work for both equations.

Answer choice (B) is the only answer that works for both equations.

If $x = 1$

then for $y = (-2 \times 1) - 1$

$y = -2 - 1$

$y = -3$

For the second equation:

$y = x - 4$

$-3 = x - 4$

$-3 + 4 = x - 4 + 4$

$-3 + 4 = x$

1 = x

26) The correct answer is A.

You need to create an equation to set out the facts of this problem. Here we will say that the total number of students is variable S.

$15 = (S - ¼S) \times ½$

$15 = ¾S \times ½$

$15 = ³/_8 S$

$15 \times 8 = ³/_8 S \times 8$

$120 = 3S$

$S = 40$

27) The correct answer is D.

Final Score = A + B + C

B = 2A

C = 3B = 3 × 2A = 6A

Now express the original equation in terms of A:

A + B + C = A + 2A + 6A = 9A

28) The correct answer is A.

For questions on systems of equations like this one, you should look at the multiplication equation first. Ask yourself, what are the factors of 24?

We know that 24 is the product of the following:

1 × 24 = 24

2 × 12 = 24

3 × 8 = 24

4 × 6 = 24

Now add each of the two factors together to solve the first equation.

1 + 24 = 25

2 + 12 = 14

3 + 8 = 11

4 + 6 = 10

(3, 8) solves both equations. Therefore, it is the correct answer.

29) The correct answer is C.

Our question stated that for all positive integers x and y: $x - 6 < 0$ and $y < x + 12$

$y < ?$

To solve inequalities like this one, you should first solve the equation for x.

$x - < 0$

$x - 6 + 6 < 0 + 6$

$x < 6$

Now solve for y by replacing x with its value.

$y < x + 12$

$y < 6 + 12$

$y < 18$

30) The correct answer is B.

Our problem asked for the solution of $2 + y < -8$

Isolate y in order to solve the problem.

$2 + y < -8$

$2 - 2 + y < -8 - 2$

$y < -10$

144
© COPYRIGHT 2008-2014. Academic Success Media DBA www.college-placement-test.com
This material may not be copied or reproduced in any form.

Made in the USA
Middletown, DE
16 March 2017